Wisdom for the New Age

New Age

TEACHINGS OF THE
GREAT WHITE BROTHERHOOD
AS GIVEN BY AZRAEL

THE NEW ANGELUS
P.O. Box 4133
W. Sedona, Arizona 86340

ISBN: 0-87516-477-3
Library of Congress Card Catalog Number: 81-85815

Distributed by
DeVorss & Company
P.O. Box 550
Marina del Rey, California 90291

Printed in the United States of America

TABLE OF CONTENTS

DEDICATION

As we approach the turn of the cycle our souls pause in wondrous anticipation before the changing events emerging from the mists of time. Piece by piece the eternal mosaic of life reforms itself from the memory bank we call experience, thereby revealing our inheritance from the Father-Mother God, the Christ Light which quickens the spark of Life Essence into being.

With deep love and gratitude we dedicate this book to The Great White Brotherhood whose devotion and guidance sustain us on our journey home to the Kingdom. In the cleansing decade that lies ahead man will reap what he has sown as our beloved Earth prepares for the coming Golden Age of peace and goodwill toward men.

Change must come, beginning and ending in the heart of each spiritual entity now bearing the cross of evolution upon his weary shoulders. Man has reached the time of decision when love for his brother is the password, and none can survive or enter the New Age without learning the magic symbol.

To Azrael, our Beloved Friend and Teacher who has shown us the gateway to the storehouse of wisdom, we bow in reverence. To Philip, his chosen channel and disciple, we give our love and gratitude.

May all who read these words be blessed and strengthened as the exciting, rewarding, spiritual adventure unfolds the pages of history in this bookmark of time!

D. E. F.

INTRODUCTION

Throughout your universe there are myriad forms of creation, most of which lie beyond the range and reach of the most powerful and sophisticated instruments of the scientists engaged in the exploration of outer space and its heavenly bodies. Indeed, it is beyond the perception of human consciousness. Yet all of this tremendous portion of God's creation, though far distant and removed from your immediate environment is, nonetheless, a part of your life and has its effect upon your life, as you do upon it.

This is a difficult fact for many to understand and to accept. But you, who seek after truth and after a better understanding of life, are better able to grasp the significance of this and more readily accept the fact that the Father does indeed know "every hair upon your head and of every sparrow that falls."

We would ask you to envision and hold in your mind, as best you can, this thought: That the farthest point of your universe, even though it may be millions and millions of miles removed from your point in it, is yet a part of it and functioning in its immediate environment in fulfillment of its purpose just as is your planet Earth functioning in its plane and orbit about the Sun of your solar system, and each planet, star, constellation and heavenly body in it is as much an integral part of this universe as is your Earth.

We would also ask that you give consideration to just how immense and great must be the powers and the energies included in and associated with both the space and the heavenly bodies that go to make up this universe. Also, imagine, if you can, the vast destruction that would follow were this universe to suddenly be thrown into a state of chaos and disharmony to the extent that all its constituent elements would be thrown from their appointed orbits and paths of movement. As you do this, you soon begin to realize that this would be a gigantic and terrible catastrophe.

But this is not the case. Your planet maintains the path assigned to it; and its moon moves about it in its assigned orbit. So do all the planets of your solar system follow their paths of orbit. Indeed you see here ample demonstration of the fact and truth that all creation has its purpose, its path, and its function, and regardless of what that function may be, each element remains in an harmonious relationship with all other parts and aspects of creation about it.

You have, no doubt, observed the harmony and balance which exists within nature. If one element fails to maintain its apparent function, or perhaps goes beyond the limits of what that function may be, events and forces are brought into action which bring it back into balance that it may carry on its assigned function. Thus harmony and balance are restored and maintained.

Perhaps you are aware of the fact that you are and represent an integral part of this universe. Indeed, the aphorism "as above, so below" shall gain ever greater meaning for you. As a microcosm in this universe, you strive to achieve the harmony and balance in your life as it exists in the macrocosm in which you dwell.

You shall find that many of our teachings express this absolute need for harmony and balance; for this is necessary if you are to bring love, wisdom, and power into your life and in proper perspective. Thus, you are encouraged to look to the fullness of life, to take the bitter with the sweet, to realize that while light brings you from darkness, without the experience of darkness you could not know the real beauty the light brings you. Thus, you learn to understand the purpose of travail, difficulty and trial; that they must be faced and overcome so the golden essence of your being shall become manifested as the dross of impurity is removed and expunged. Only then may the beautiful light of the Christ within, with Its radiance as bright and as strong and as pure as the light of your Sun, shine forth.

Therefore, we remind you always to remember that while it is wise to seek after knowledge, it is much wiser to concern yourself with the simple virtue of giving of self into the needs of others. This is a mystery in its own right, nevertheless, we would have you know that always when one gives to his fellow man the love which lies within his heart, he gives of what God has given him, thus manifesting the Divine Self in form and effective expression upon this plane of life. When this occurs, you find that all else we have said above also become active and effective principles in your life.

God seeks to manifest His Presence and His Power through you just as He does through us, your discarnate invisible brethren. When you allow this to happen, the power of the Christ is made manifest and automatically the forces and powers which bring harmony, peace and balance flow into your life. You strive after perfection, and though that perfection is yet a long way off, you must not be discouraged in the slightest.

Look to the beautiful story told by the Master Jesus in the parable of the Prodigal Son. You can see there the demonstration of the ever-present power of the Father's love. Recall how it was that as the son began his return to his Father, and while "yet a long way off," the Father came out to meet him and placed his arms about him and kissed him. Perhaps you can see why we stress the importance of your giving of your love. Indeed, the Father gives abundantly and freely of His love unto you, but He means for you to do likewise; indeed you must.

Yes, dearly beloved brethren, just as must the farthest heavenly body of your universe give obedience to its assigned function and path, so, too, must you give obedience to the laws which govern your path — the path of love, light and truth. You strive after fulfillment of this purpose and ultimately you shall achieve it in glorification of the Father's Presence within you.

AZRAEL

WISDOM FOR THE NEW AGE

Chapter 1

THE WORK, BOOK, AND PURPOSES
OF THE MESSAGES

You have been led to this moment.

THE work of the Great White Brotherhood continues, as it shall continue throughout eternity. The form, the place, the plane, these all may change, but the divine truths which lie at the base and are the foundation of all things shall always remain the same. The immutable Law of God remains inviolate, never to be changed, even by God. And what is this Law, save the manifestation of love in every form? The Law of God is just, it is right, it is proper, it is fair. All equity and goodness is its reward. Man has sought throughout the ages to change it and its application into the affairs of man but to no avail, for lo, the love of God overshadows and overcomes all that would suppress it or destroy it.

The work of the Great White Brotherhood takes on many forms at times. There are times when it is difficult for man to understand how it may come to pass that certain things occur when and where they do. Frequently there are occurrences which lead to doubt, scepticism, disbelief. Many times the changes which are brought to bear are really not the wish of the Brotherhood, but are made necessary because of the will of man—your will. For this, too, is a part of the immutable Law of God: Free will, the right to free thought, this gift of God to all men shall also remain inviolate.

This work you do now, and which you shall continue to do, in part comes by reason of certain happenings

1

brought about through change; yet, all the while, these events were, in a sense, predestined. You have been led to this moment as you shall be led to many other such moments of contact with the work of the Brotherhood. This is your choice, for were it not your choice, you would not be here, nor would those who read these words be reading them. Indeed, dearly beloved, you are about your Father's business.

We bless you, dearly beloved, and with the Grace of the Father are we permitted to have communion with you, our dear brethren, upon the plane of life in which you now dwell. And this form of communication being available to us, we seek to serve several purposes by it. First, and perhaps foremost, is the purpose of edification, of our being permitted this opportunity to bring to you these teachings we have received from the Beloved Master who has directed that they be delivered in such form as to be more easily discerned and understood by all who come upon them. It is our hope that they shall be taken into your hearts and be made an active part of your life.

We realize, of course, that what we say may not necessarily be in agreement with all you may presently hold to. It may disagree with concepts you have long subscribed to and find more acceptable. On the other hand, it may be that the concepts you have are in keeping with levels of understanding above those which appear to be included in what we teach. We would have you know this, however: That while there is carried within our words the intendments and meanings and teachings obviously presented by such words, there also lie within them additional and deeper meanings. Perhaps they are hidden, or included as a subtle meaning carried beneath the language expressed, but, in all events, it is for your consciousness, through the medium of your intellect and your heart, to discern them, to understand them, and, of course, to make them a part of your consciousness and an active force in your life.

Because of this fact, we suggest that you reread these messages and these teachings frequently. And not only those which we give through this channel, Philip, but also those we have earlier given through our beloved Roselady.

Truth is truth and forever shall it be the truth, wherever it is found. Man's understanding and realization of it is necessarily limited by his ability to perceive of it. But as his insight and awareness and the unfoldment of his Higher Self progresses from day to day, if not from moment to moment, so, too, does his ability to perceive of new understanding and realization change and become clearer. It is this element of change within yourself which is both encouraged and desired.

Another purpose served through this means of communion is the opportunity to pass on to you the beautiful joy of hope eternal. This hope is not in any sense an attitude or feeling as would be conceived in despair, rather, it is a form of realization grounded in truth, faith, enlightenment, courage, strength, goodness and righteousness to the highest degree you can presently comprehend. It is in many respects the source of your motivation to seek after higher levels of consciousness. And this, beloved brethren, is also an aspect of God's Principle of Creation being made manifest in you. For the fire of the spirit within you which is constant in its drive to have you do these things is never dormant, nor is it intended to be. Indeed, this Power of Creation is an ever ongoing power in your life, as at all levels of life, from the highest to the lowest form of life. Thus you find that your life is indeed a part of this phenomenon; that you grow, evolve and ascend ever higher upon the spiral of life.

We find joy in being permitted this privilege to serve the purposes in part enumerated here. We see that you find joy in them also and your hope is renewed and strengthened. You are blessed in the never ending abundance of the love of the Father-Mother God which is within you and with which we bless you, now and always.

Chapter 2

THE LIGHT, THE PATH, AND THE PURPOSE

THE LIGHT

The light of your hearts, my beloved brethren, is a beautiful spectacle and sight to see. For this truly is the Perfect Light—the light of the Father-Mother God—the Christ Light which dwells within the hearts of all men.

THE Christ light is waiting to be used, to be released and expressed in the form of thoughts, words, and deeds of love. This light—divine love—is the power of the universe.

Your thoughts send forth a light, the quality of which is determined by and is equal to the nature of your thoughts. The words you speak also send forth a light, its quality also being determined by the quality of what is being spoken. And so, too, do your actions issue forth a light, the quality of which is similarly determined.

We speak in this way that you would be more aware of the role this power we call "light" plays in your life and of its continuous presence and involvement in your life.

Whenever you think a thought, say a word, or do any act, you both use and express a form of energy. And even if the form of that expression should be low in spiritual value, it is, nevertheless, a utilization of that energy. Therefore, the purer the form of the expression coming

4

from you, the more radiant the light flowing from it can be, for purity is its inherent nature.

The teachings of the Beloved Master, Jesus, as with the teachings of all Masters, concentrate upon the need of man to learn to live a more godlike life; bringing the principles of truth into his daily living and affairs. We, too, seek to bring these teachings before you with great frequency, even as now, for it is so necessary for you to learn this; that you would express in your life, in your daily living, the pure White Light of God's Presence within you.

The greater the light you express and radiate becomes of that quality, the stronger and more vibrant and powerful it shall be. And the more meaningful it shall be, not only to your life, but to the lives of all those to whom you may reach and touch with your life.

In your external earthly world the most commonly accepted and understood form of communication is that of word and action. Upon the invisible inner planes, my beloved brethren, communication is made through the power of thought, and this form of transference of idea or information gives a means for a more complete impartation and clarity of understanding and communion. Thus we know your thoughts, and, to a substantial degree, so also does your own inner self receive the thoughts of others, as they receive your thoughts.

No doubt, you have never paused to give attention to the realization of how many thoughts you bring to mind and entertain but do not express in word or deed. Obviously, without making any calculation or count, you immediately realize that the number of thoughts you entertain and hold in your mind far outnumber those you express externally.

Nevertheless, a thought is an expression and use of energy, and the process of the mind which matures into a thought completes, to that extent, that expression of energy. Thus a thought brought forth in that capacity alone is a completed form of expression of the self that has issued it forth. Its nature, its quality, its effect is communicated and expressed upon the invisible planes, and you must realize that your thoughts are indeed commitments you make even though they may not become expressed at that point into the external world. Their effect ultimately does become manifest. Remember, that which is expressed within shall become expressed in the outer self—"As within, so without."

Hence, it should be exceedingly clear why we suggest and teach "Practicing the Presence" of God in all your activities, and especially as this applies to the use of your mind to the commitment of thought.

The Beloved Master teaches: "Ye are the light of the world." And indeed you are; but the brilliance of your light is determined by that which you choose to express.

The light of love, the light of knowledge, the light of wisdom, constantly surrounds and enfolds you, and, to the extent that you let it, buoys you up, supports you, and carries you gently as if you were in the arms of the Father, being held gently, yet surely and protectively in the power of the divine love of the Father's Grace.

It is your responsibility to take within and into your being as much of this light as you possibly can. We would give you an example. Were you to submerge yourself in a body of water, diving beneath the surface, you would of course be completely surrounded by the water, would you not? But unless and until you opened your nostrils or your mouth and permitted the water to enter your body, it would have no effect upon your innerself, except for the pressures that it would bring against your body externally.

So, too, with the light of the Father's Divine Presence. While there is the Light of the Christ within you, there is also more about you. And if you picture yourself as being immersed in a total sea of White Light, yet keeping yourself closed off from it, except for that effect flowing from its mere presence — perhaps somewhat as a process of osmosis — you would receive very little of it until you opened yourself to it.

In other words, there must be the conscious intended effort to open yourself to the realization and the grace of the Father's Presence, and this effort must come from you.

It is the creative power of the thoughts of men that brings into form universal substance which may be useful and necessary in their human lives. Thus man is enabled to create from divine substance that which may be useful, both to meet his personal needs and to bring into fulfillment God's will for him.

The validity of this statement may inspire debate in some circles, and be immediately questioned in others, because of the many forms of human activity which, obviously, harbor and foster evil purpose in myriad forms. Our response to such argument and questioning would be: You must look beyond and beneath only the surface or external form of these activities to the ultimate values they may bring into the lives of everyone involved.

The light of the Christ is within each of you. It has been covered over, no doubt, in many, and, in some, to a great depth by the darkness of ignorance and the corruption of evil thought, deed, and desire. But this does not mean that this Light of God is no longer present within, or that it has been extinguished. Indeed, it has not been, nor shall it ever be.

Someday, somewhere, in some incarnation — if not this one, and in each one, to a degree — at the appropriate moment, the light within shall become quickened and be born anew to grow and to unfold, bit by bit, step by step. Ultimately, it shall become a beautiful radiance, as beautiful and as radiant as that light manifested by the Beloved Master Jesus.

This is the destiny of man, as it is your destiny. If there is any among you who cannot take heart and strength and courage in this, then, indeed, you are condemned to a long period in darkness and despair. But even you shall ultimately find your radiant destiny in life; for the light within is eternal in its presence and in its purpose.

Herein lies one of the many reasons why the beloved Master Jesus taught as He did upon the principle of forgiveness and gave often of the admonition not to pass judgment upon others. For each of you is indeed, a child of God, blessed by the Presence of the Father and of the strength of that inheritance already vested within each of you.

Thus you learn to use the Light of the Father's Presence. With this Light which is within you, which glows brilliantly and radiantly—for it is the love of God waiting to be expressed in love and harmony—you shall attain fulfillment of your quest for spiritual unfoldment. Let your light shine, beloved brethren, let its limitless power and beauty lighten your path unto the Father.

THE PATH

Thy word is a lamp unto my feet, and a light unto my path. (Psalms 119:105)

This verse of the Psalm tells what the hearts of men have known throughout the ages. Even now your hearts know this and give thanks unto the Father-Mother God for the guidance which has placed you upon the path you follow to the Light of Truth.

While men's actions belie the true nature of their being, through the manifestation of the evil and negative actions naturally flowing from the darkness of the ignorance in which they seemingly are content to remain bound, deep within, hidden beneath the human outer self, there lies a longing for the light—the Light of Truth. And it is the longing, this eternal inherent quality of the soul, which ultimately breaks through the bonds of darkness enough to allow the Light of the Word to enter into the mind of the heart and quicken the dormant light of the Spirit within.

Sooner or later, this occurrence comes into the life of every soul. It has been described and defined in numerous ways. Perhaps the most adequate is that given by the Master Jesus when he explained to Nicodemus that for man to enter into the kingdom of Heaven he must "be born again;" that without this phenomenon of regeneration his path of life and being would not progress into the Light. Indeed, it is from this beginning, this "spark which quickens the spirit," that all men come to find the path which shall lead them to the realization and understanding of truth as the real substance of their lives. Thus there begin to function those processes which shall enable the soul to gain deeper insight into the need for the development of relationships with others which provide the means for a more complete fulfillment of purpose.

Your present understanding of the concept of "duality of being," and its paramount sense of "individuality," is the normal and natural result of your spiritual unfoldment up to this point in life. Indeed, you are where you are, and the degree of intelligence and wisdom you possess is determined by what you have earlier done to earn and achieve your present level of consciousness and understanding. And while your present conditions may cause or tend to produce some difficulty for you, they are, nevertheless, a substantial improvement over what they were. Moreover, you observe that your growth to this point is measured by how well you have followed the light placed upon your path. We seek now, as always, to add to that light.

This concept is also a fertile seedbed for the powerful and destructive negative trait you know and define as "selfishness." This one characteristic creates and is responsible for most, if not all, of your problems. It is, perhaps, the greatest obstacle you presently face. Yet, it is a natural part of your life, and is meant to be the nemesis it is. Without it, you would not have the opportunities for evolvement that it, and the environment it creates, gives you. It, like all else involved in your existence, has a definite and needed purpose in your life. But, just because it brings you these needed experiences, this does not mean that you should continue to harbor or nurture this quality of character. Rather, the challenges it produces are to be confronted and experienced, ultimately to be overcome and replaced with its opposite quality of "selflessness." Thus you grow and continue your spiritual unfoldment.

As you reflect upon our words, you may more clearly perceive of the substantial power and impact your acceptance of the misconceptions flowing from the illusory forces and conditions of the earth plane have had upon you, especially blocking you from the self-realization and insight as to the true nature of your being and your relationships with others. And because you have become so accustomed to believe in external things, and the influence they may have, it is difficult for you to consistently adhere to those practices needed to penetrate the earthly facade and to help unfold the true Self of the Spirit that dwells within you.

Obviously, you are seeking after greater understanding and knowledge of yourself and of your purposes in life, otherwise you would not be interested in what we give you through these means. Indeed, you would be interested in other things. Even so, it is wise for you to be vigilant and guard against any weakness which may arise to interfere with your spiritual progress.

For example, it is helpful to anticipate the need to reinforce your commitment to spiritual purposes, for you may find yourself involved in situations in which you are hard pressed to remain loyal to this commitment. If this occurs, do not let the adversity of the moment become stronger than it is by belaboring it with undue concern and anxiety. Nor should you be critical of yourself for having become involved in this experience, unless, of course, you recognize your situation and then fail to do anything about changing it for the better. The main point we seek to make here is that you should not be surprised to find yourself making this kind of mistake. Indeed, look at what happened to the great Apostle Peter. Peter even bragged to the Master of his ability and his power always to remain loyal in his commitment to the Master, yet he denied Him thrice, as the Master predicted he would.

You know that often you are tested. Sometimes the tests are very difficult, but each time you meet a test and hold fast to your spiritual commitment and purpose, a remarkable strengthening of your faith ensues. Indeed, the strength of your faith is the foundation and strength of your commitment in the first place, and it is upon this virtue that you are thus enabled to build a beautiful power for good in your life.

The Purpose

All of life has its purpose indeed. All of life is a beautiful outworking of the Father's Law and His Love. Let this truth be the source of everlasting joy in your hearts.

There run through the minds of many of you thoughts concerning your contributions to life. In some respects it is good that you do this, in others, it is perhaps not wise that you do so. We would speak briefly upon this from the standpoint of helping you to direct your thoughts in such a way as to perhaps give you greater insight into yourselves. We do not, of course, seek to control your thoughts, nor in any way to interfere with your freedom of thought, but we would make these suggestions in the form of guidance to you.

It is an entirely normal process for you to wish and to feel that what you do in this life is for a good purpose, not only to yourselves but to all those around you, the members of your family, your friends and your associates and those you meet from day to day. There are times, however, that you may find yourself becoming too engrossed in concern over this aspect of life which, in turn, may inspire the ego to become too ambitious in controlling the mechanism which cultivates your attitudes and ambitions. While it is not wrong to be ambitious and anxious to do good and bring fulfillment into one's life, attitudes too strongly fixed in that direction give rise to corresponding tendencies to be overly critical of oneself, even to the point that such self-criticism may get entirely out of hand.

Perhaps it is a form of paradox, nevertheless, we find frequently that such an individual is his most severe critic; and all too often, unfortunately, this occurs to those who are becoming more sensitive to life. Indeed, the efforts you now make to achieve greater spiritual awareness necessarily bring an increase in your own sensitivities. As you have found from your own experiences, the fact that you are making a sincere and honest investigation into truth and the deeper meanings of life and your relationship with them, causes you to become more sensitive to the forces and influences about you, which you encounter daily both from without and from within. And you shall learn, if you have not already done so, that as you grow in such sensitivity—and this will occur as you come into attunement with the vibrations on higher levels of consciousness—there also arises within you the possibility of becoming overly sensitive.

This latter development may open you to an attitude or feeling which is negative in nature, and one which you must try to avoid, but there is yet another possibility which requires even greater concern. That has to do with self-criticism, which can develop to the point of pulling you down into a valley of depression from which it may be quite difficult to arise. This is another reason why we speak frequently upon the principle of harmony and balance and of the constant need to invoke the principle of love and brotherhood, the giving of self, and adopting, as best one can, those attitudes which are motivated only by desire for selflessness. When so motivated and so directed, the individual will find himself steered away from the brink of darkness and despair which emerges from and is cultivated by exaggerated self-criticism and the feeling of guilt.

If you find yourself entertaining questioning thoughts such as: "Am I really accomplishing anything? Am I fulfilling my purposes in life? Am I making any spiritual progress at all?" We would assure you, beloved brethren, the answer is, "Yes, indeed you are!"

Life is not a vacuum. You are not reading these words through any accident or through happenstance. You, our beloved incarnate brethren, are at this moment engaged in this activity because you are seeking to fulfill purposes chosen by your spiritual self to be fulfilled. All the events that have gone before have led to this moment; and those which are to come shall build the circumstances, conditions, and events of the tomorrows. As you strive after fulfillment of these purposes, and to meet well your responsibilities, you benefit because of your interest in your spiritual values and by endeavoring to learn better of what it is that you are to do.

It is the matter of becoming overly concerned and overly critical of yourself and of the way you are responding to the challenges of life that we would have you guard against. You are well aware of the need to heed the admonition of the beloved Master Jesus not to make judgment or criticism of others and to forgive freely their transgressions against you. There lies within each of you an equally strong need to avoid making such judgment and criticisms of yourself which go beyond the perimeters of honest self-appraisal and correction of character defects; and that you also be willing to forgive yourself your mistakes. We assume, of course, that you will not allow yourself to rationalize these statements to the point that you may justify actions which you know, or should know, to be wrong and contrary to your spiritual purposes. The thrust of this teaching is to help you to avoid the unwitting temptation yielded to by so many to allow their ego to slide into and languish within the throes of self-pity. Yes, dearly beloved, you must not judge others, but also learn not to judge yourselves too harshly.

It is not always easy for man to see and to understand what his real purposes may be; and why it is that the trials that befall him would come about in the way they do. Frequently, he cries out in distress, asking why he should have such suffering and tribulation. And a response which says: "This is given to you that you would learn and come to understand more fully your purposes in life" is rejected as being merely a cliché of little strength or hope. Yet, dear brethren, this is no platitude, nor is it intended as an effort to avoid a deeper explanation of why these things must occur in your life. The reasons why we cannot go beyond certain limits in what we may disclose to you shall become increasingly evident as you move along your path. Indeed, if the reasons or causes for every challenge and test you encounter were immediately or prematurely disclosed, their effectiveness as learning experiences would be substantially lessened, if not completely destroyed.

Think back objectively to earlier experiences in this in-carnation and you shall recall that those experiences which presented the most difficulty and gave you the greatest concern, and which you had to work with the hardest, produced the most valuable learning experi-ences of lasting impression. Indeed, they added much to your knowledge, wisdom and understanding. It was the difficulty, the trial, the effort required to meet and over-come what lay before you that brought a rewarding sense of achievement and a greater appreciation of your ability to obtain a resolution of those problems. On the other hand, the problems which were easy to cope with presented opportunities of far less meaning and value, from the standpoint of serving as learning experiences.

Illness, and other like experiences, leave their impres-sions and effect upon the soul, giving it every such ex-perience it may need to have. Not a single event comes into your life without cause or purpose. All life has conti-nuity, all life has purpose, everything has its place and its order of fulfillment. Each event and circumstance serves both as the expression of an effect from an earlier cause or causes, and as a producing cause of that which is to be later expressed. Yet all these processes, and their order of development and expression, are governed primarily by your individual power of free will and freedom of choice. What you will and choose to bring into your life, deter-mines your path.

That which is generally expressed as your life now, dearly beloved, has resulted from what has gone before and shall, by operation of law, be productive of what shall be expressed tomorrow and, perhaps, even many years from now. Each thought, each word, each deed, produces its effect which must come into manifestation at its appropriate time.

This Law or Principle of Cause and Effect, while de-manding and precise in its application, is, as it is with all things that flow from God, designed to develop and bring forth the good which is in all men. Indeed, were it not for its effectiveness, man would likely remain forever a victim of the undisciplined nature of his being. There would not evolve the disciplinary processes naturally flowing from the effectiveness of this law that places him on the path of light and truth; and then keeps him there once he has found it. Nor does it require man to, in any way, forfeit his gift of free will; this remains forever his inviolate right and privilege, subject only to his being responsible for the effects of his actions, upon himself and upon others.

All things God has given you, and continues to give you, are given in love. They are good and are meant to be used for good. They are of His love, given in love, that you may learn to manifest that love in every part of your life. The energies of this universe are a form of this gift and you are to have them for your use in gaining fulfillment of your purposes in life.

The power of the thoughts you engender, whether they dwell with you for a time, or are expressed in word or other form of action, has its source among these invisible energies. Perhaps it would help you to understand this process better if we used a form of metaphor. Let us compare these energies to the waters of a fresh pure stream. Perhaps the stream has its source in an underground spring, appearing as a never ending source of supply. As the water first comes forth it is clear, pure, cool and so very refreshing, quenching quickly the thirst of all who drink from it. Then, as it flows along its course, changes begin to occur. All along its way it contributes to the life and sustenance of plants, animals, and, perhaps, human life. It may also serve as the source of power and energy for industrial plants, water works, and hydro-electrical plants. It may even serve to carry vessels of all kinds. At certain points, it may become polluted and its purity lessened substantially.

It may ultimately reach a larger body of water, a lake, bay, or ocean. Here, the process of evaporation may lift it gently into the skies, forming into clouds, to be allowed to fall back again to Earth in some form of precipitation; or, through the process of osmosis or by underground rivers and streams, it may find its way back to the spring from which it first came. In each instance, however, it passes through a cycle, a cycle of use and of service.

The energies that empower your thoughts pass through cycles, very similar in nature. At their source they are pure. Their use and the degree to which they may retain their purity depends upon the use you make of them. You, therefore, determine whether these energies shall become polluted by evil thoughts, or improper use, or whether they shall be used to give life to good, positive thoughts of helpful, useful and creative purposes beneficial to mankind as a whole. But whatever the use you make of them, the energies per se return to their original status and source, while the effects you created from them ultimately return to you.

All uses of energy are cyclic in nature, and the energy is never lost or wasted. Indeed, it provides a means of power for the evolution of all creation, of all forms of life. Thus, you have another demonstration of the fact that all forms and all beings are in some way connected with everything else.

Just as your life, and what you do with it, affects others outside and beyond yourself, so do the lives of others affect you. There is no escaping this truth, not to the slightest degree. If you are joyful, your joy affects, in a similar way, all others within the influence of your being. If you are sad, your sadness similarly affects others.

Far too many do not realize that the power and influence of their mind expressed in thoughts and other actions reaches far beyond their immediate environment. Little do they realize the extent of their effect; that it may be substantial. So, if we seem to lay emphasis upon this matter of your disciplining your thoughts, of your being aware of the power they hold and convey, understand, beloved brethren, that we do so for good purpose and reason.

Your life, and how you use it is important, not only to yourself, but to all your brethren; and, especially, to God. At times you may feel very small and insignificant in the vast expanse of your universe, but you must not allow yourself to dwell upon this kind of thinking, for you are as much an essential part of the whole, as is every other part and being. As your awareness and understanding increase, your powers of spiritual perception shall also increase and, in time, the realization of these truths shall reach your consciousness and you will *know* that this is so!

Indeed, it is your chosen purpose to gain in such knowledge and spiritual comprehension, and it is our function to aid you as best we can in your spiritual quest. We place before you teachings which give you light and truth which shall strengthen your trust and faith in the love of the Blessed Father-Mother God. Indeed, our immediate purpose is to give you, to the utmost, our love, our strength, and to encourage you to move forward with enthusiasm and confidence, blessed always by God's love.

Profit by learning from everything you do. Know that today you are in the environment you have earned, and know also that tomorrow will bring into your life the persons and events which have similarly been earned. Even though you are called upon to face circumstances and conditions which can be very trying and difficult, all of them are the result of your previous actions and are designed to teach you lessons needed to be learned.

The Master Jesus teaches you how to obtain the fullness of life for which all men seek. He also teaches the principle of living a day at a time; and so do we. Indeed, that which occurred yesterday is beyond your control. The effects produced by what occurred then have already been set into motion. What is to come tomorrow is not yet here, but what you do today affects both what is to be your life for this day, and, together with what has gone before, shall in great measure determine what your tomorrow shall be. But whatever tomorrow may hold for you, when it becomes "today" cherish every moment of it and do the best you know how to do to demonstrate your true heritage as a child of God; indeed, this should be your goal for each day.

The privilege of choice is always yours to make. This is an important aspect of freedom of will which the Father has entrusted to us all. And this power is within the sole power of each one to use. Thus it should be very evident why we take such joy as we do when we witness you, our beloved brethren, making choices which lead to the unfoldment of your spiritual essence.

Chapter 3

PERSEVERANCE

Ask, and it shall be given you; seek, and ye shall find; knock, and it shall be opened unto you.
(Matthew 7:7; Luke 11:9)

Thy kingdom of heaven opens unto all who truly seek after it. May there come from these dear souls the asking, the seeking, and the knocking that Thy kingdom may be opened unto them.

IT IS through perseverance that you continue in your search after truth, the light which guides all men to the throne of God—that ultimate point in life when all shall again be as one with the Father. And while that time may yet be a far way off, this is no cause for you to make any less effort to gain deeper insight into these truths and make application of them to the actions and needs of your daily living. For you are meant to seek and to gain a greater awareness and understanding of your true spiritual nature.

As you take cognizance of the purposes which motivate you, you are helped immensely in making the choices you must make to direct you into gaining a deeper understanding of what your relationship to life really amounts to. In fact, this may be your first real step in that direction.

There are many who carefully study your Bible, and other spiritual writings, and believe that by having fixed firmly into their minds the knowledge derived from such sources they have grown substantially in spiritual stature. In a way, this practice can be helpful, but there is more to true spiritual growth than that.

Intellectual spiritual attainment is not enough, dear brethren. Your soul desires the spiritual perfection as manifested by Jesus the Christ. Intellectual attainment alone will not do this. It is helpful and important, yes, and we do not discourage you from studying spiritual and inspirational material, but your spiritual growth must go beyond the intellectual level. The knowledge you gain of spiritual truth must reach your heart, to the center of your being, that it shall guide your will and your actions. There must be an *assimilation* of truth to the point that it becomes the active focus of your life.

It has been correctly stated that to know of and to speak of love is vastly different from living love, giving love, and being a manifestation of love. Look to the life of the Master Jesus. He not only taught the principles of love, He lived and demonstrated them fully for all men to see and to emulate. And so must you learn to bring forth the Christ within. Sooner or later, you shall, and when you do, you will serve as as example to your fellow-man of what it is like to make love the fulcrum about which your life pivots.

This is why we present these matters to you in this way. Perhaps these teachings are stated simply, but they are given in a way that all who read them may find in them a form of guidance which can materially change their lives for the better.

But again, they are of no value to you, or to anyone else, until they are used and practiced. No one can do this for you. Each one serves to be his own salvation to the extent that he may fulfill his purposes in life and attain total spiritual unfoldment.

We have selected a theme from the recorded words of our Master, Jesus the Christ, which carry a profound and

significant message to all who would look for the inner
meanings given in them.

We shall set forth meanings which we believe are intended by them. However, we remind you of our position
in making presentations of this nature. We do not take
the position that what we say is the only interpretation,
meaning, or significance which you may receive from the
teachings of Jesus. Indeed, we merely demonstrate to you
how you may find deeper meanings and teachings which
can be gleaned from the words of the Master. Taking only the literal meaning, and stopping there, gives but a
limited understanding, and often proves to be grossly in-
adequate for one who would be a "Seeker" after Truth
and who would be a true disciple of the Master Jesus.

This teaching is found reported in your Bible in both
gospels of Matthew and Luke in the same context exactly; this alone is somewhat unusual and worthy of note.

Three separate forms of action are suggested for you to
take, should you wish to obtain "heavenly things from the
Father." You must *ask, seek,* and *knock.* Since these actions are given together in a conjunctive manner, rather
than separately, or disjunctively, we consider this an important suggestion to look closely for the keys which may
be present with which to unlock any hidden or subtle di-
rectives and guidance.

We point out that Jesus frequently, if not always, gave
His deeper teachings in the form of a parable or an alle-
gory. Bearing this in mind, we shall examine the passages
which appear both before and after the particular pas-
sage we are studying to see if we may find anything there
which shall add to our understanding of it.

We find in Luke's account of this teaching, there is a
parable immediately preceding it which appears to give
significant definition to what we are looking for. As we
read this parable, we find that it tells a very simple story
of one who has gone to a friend at a very late hour of the
night seeking to borrow three loaves of bread that he may

give food to a friend who "in his journey, is come to me and I have nothing to set before him." And, in response to his plea, he hears his friend answering from within that he does not wish to be troubled, that the door is now shut, all have gone to bed, and he cannot get up and give him the bread. But as it is stated, "Though he will not rise and give him, because he is his friend; yet because of his importunity, he will rise and give him as many as he needeth."

From the parable, we immediately see that the teaching is stressing the importance of persistence. While the friend would not rise from his bed and give the loaves to his neighbor out of friendship alone, he would arise, finally, to answer the persistent importuning of his neighbor.

Thus, Jesus is adding this emphasis to His teaching, that each one must be persistent in his "asking, seeking, and knocking." This gives you an important teaching, however, we examine further into the parable to see if there are additional meanings of value and assistance.

The teachers of the Ancient Wisdom followed extensively the practice of using symbols in their teachings. This also is the practice of the Master Jesus, so, it is appropriate for us to examine this parable in that light.

We suggest that the various items and identities employed in the parable have additional symbolical value. For example: The "three loaves" may represent a significant reference to the Trinity, the Three in One, the Divine Source of the food that feeds the soul and the spirit. The "friend of mine" obviously symbolizes the soul, and "his journey" represents the path it has chosen for spiritual growth. "He from within" represents the Higher Self—the Presence and the Power of the Father which dwells within each one. The "door" represents the Christ Way, the correct path to the Source. For as Jesus said, "I am the Way, the Truth, and the Life; no man cometh unto the Father, but by me." "At midnight" symbolizes a time of darkness, the darkness which surrounds the soul which has not yet become aware of the Christ Light which already lies within its heart.

Now using these symbols, but in the context of the matters they represent, we shall again go through the parable and determine if other teachings may be discovered.

There is a time in the life of every one when the soul becomes "quickened" and consciously aware of its need for the food of divine truth beyond that which it has so far found upon its journey—the path which ultimately returns to the Father-Mother God. As such awareness increases, there comes about a realization that the source it seeks is the Source within. And thus its quest begins in earnest. But it finds the door is shut and does not freely open to it. In time it learns that through importunity, through persistent and repeated asking, seeking, and knocking, the door finally opens and the soul is given of the food it needs.

Perhaps you now understand that Jesus is saying to you, "If you are to receive for your soul the truths which flow from God, and are to move ever onward and upward towards attainment of that spiritual posture which gives spiritual perfection, you must remain constant and persistent in your efforts."

Now we shall examine carefully the three actions this teaching demands of you, if you wish to grow spiritually. They apparently require three different forms of action, however, we believe an analysis of them shall result in the conclusion that they are substantially interrelated. Yet, in the sense intended, each of them meets a specific need necessary to equip you with the tools you must have to help you achieve greater spiritual awareness.

You will note that apparently the Beloved Master gives this teaching as a part of the teaching generally being given to his disciples to aid them in their own spiritual endeavors. We would think that you should keep this in mind as you make your own study of this material and of the Master's teachings as well.

What first comes to mind with the term *ask*? It seems that prayer fits best into this category of suggested action. Prayer is used, of course, to give praise and thanksgiving to God, but primarily it is used as a means of presenting your wishes, desires, petitions and requests to the Father. Just as you ask of others that they would honor your requests, so, too, do you go to the Father in prayer that your requests of Him may be answered and granted. The exact form that this action may take is not necessarily the controlling factor. The important thing is that you have recognized your need, that you have a need that can only be filled through the help of God, and you are "asking" for His help.

To *seek* is to search for something, to find that which is hidden from you. In this context, we believe you will agree that this pertains to a search for truth. As used here, it also includes the study and analysis of the content of your Bible, and such other spiritual and philosophical writings to which you are led, searching out answers to the questions you find rising from your inner self. As you follow this practice of "seeking" you shall find a corresponding growth in your ability to discern and recognize the knowledge which best fills your present needs. Thus you learn to cull out and discard those ideas and tenets which may deter your spiritual progress, or which may cause harm to your spiritual well-being. Obviously, progress in these areas adds breadth to your level of consciousness and awareness generally.

"*Knock*, and it shall be opened to you." We believe no one would doubt the assurance this gives that as you knock at the door which opens to your Higher Self, ultimately your knocking shall open this "door of the Christ" and Its Light shall become the guiding light of all you do. For remember, Jesus said, "I am the door: by me if any man enter in, he shall be saved." In an earlier discussion of the import of this latter statement of the Master, we suggested this to mean that it is through the practice of meditation that you are given the means to reach the Source of your spiritual food. By such practice you learn to "enter through the door" of the Higher Self—the Christ within—into the kingdom of Heaven where you receive guidance and sustenance for your spiritual needs.

We say, therefore, that this term "knock" symbolizes the practice of meditation. It is through this practice that you gain entrance into the highest part of your Spiritual Self. You thus find the pathway which takes you to the "mountain top" where you may be lifted into the Blinding Presence of the Almighty.

It is clear from this teaching, however, that the practice of meditation should not be used to the exclusion of either of the other practices of prayer (asking) and study (seeking). Were this intended, Jesus would not have included the three forms of action together as He did. Indeed, dear brethren, each action has its importance, each has its place, and each has its need. You are to give attention to them all, if you are to move forward in your quest after spiritual perfection.

For example, the time devoted to prayer, dearly beloved, brings you much happiness. Indeed, you sense a deep feeling of peace; and this should be, for at such times you are also reaching to the "stillness and quiet within."

There are many who do not yet realize that as they enter into prayer, selflessly, in love and for divine purpose, the Presence of the Divine within is invoked and joins Its force to such prayer, giving it much power and strength. Selfless prayer allows you to become a channel for God's Love and Power to bless and heal others.

Although the statement, "Ask, and it shall be given you" would hint at exclusive personal type prayers, we repeat what we have earlier said: Let your prayers be selfless and in aspiration to the All-wise Eternal Spirit of

Love and Light, and in the endeavor to come into closer at-one-ment and attunement with the Father's Will so that the Christ, the Son, may truly become an active force in your life.

As you continue in this form of "asking," you experience spiritual attainment in your own right, although this is not the motivating cause of your action. Changes come very subtly in and to your character and, frequently, to your environment as well. These may be difficult to recognize at first, nevertheless, they do come about. As these changes occur, you are prompted even more by an inner urging to seek after activities and avenues which allow you an even greater opportunity for the giving of self in love to your fellow man. And each such action causes a like or similar effect, bringing into your consciousness an ever-increasing awareness of spiritual values.

Thus, you feed your soul and give it nourishment steeped in spiritual nutrition that helps it to grow and to ascend to higher levels of awareness and being. And with each step taken, a closer relationship is drawn between the actions advocated by this teaching of Jesus. Thus, you shall regularly employ these tools in your endeavor to live a more Christlike life. Then are the promises of this teaching fulfilled. For as you have asked, you receive; and as you seek, you find; and as you knock, there has been opened unto you the way that you may learn of the deeper Hidden Mysteries.

But revelation of the mysteries and the light of the Ancient Wisdom shall only come to those who follow in the Way of the Christ. The laws of God are precise in their workings. You reap only that which you have sown. Thus the mysteries of the Inner Truths are not revealed to any one who has not earned this right. Jesus admonishes his disciples not to give of these teachings "unto the dogs, neither cast ye your pearls before swine, lest they trample them under their feet, and turn again and rend you."

The undeserving, the unprepared, little appreciate the beauty of these Truths. Moreover, there is the danger that they may attempt to pervert them and use them for evil purposes.

Truly, beloved brethren, the wise heed the urgings of their souls and dutifully set out to find the "three loaves" that their souls may be fed and nourished. And may each of you aspire to do likewise. As you carry forward this responsibility as one of love, you shall experience an inner peace and joy which shall transmute your struggles into aspirations, sorrows into happiness, resentments into love, and darkness into light. These rewards are awaiting you, dear ones, awaiting all who would but take of God's love and give it unto his brother.

Chapter 4

PEACE—OUTPOURING OF LOVE

Peace I Leave With You; My Peace I Give To You,
Not As The World Gives Do I Give To You.
(John 14:27)

True Harmony, and Thus True Peace, Comes
Through The Gift of Thy Love.

WE BEGIN by asking if you have ever considered the full import of the meaning to be given to this statement of the Master Jesus. As you begin to do this, we suggest that you do so with the attitude and understanding that the meaning and impact of these words, though given nearly two thousand years ago, have as much meaning and application to you now, at this moment in your lives, as when they were first spoken. With this in mind, we ask you to consider: What is this "peace" that the Christ leaves with you and gives to you?

We believe this investigation is aided through finding a definition of "peace" which gives a meaning most acceptable to your soul. And, for the time being at least, we believe this should be the privilege of each one. That is, that each of you should place your own definition to this term and use that understanding of it which brings you the most meaningful explanation and significance it can. We now set before you guidelines you may wish to follow.

By way of general definition, peace has been defined as being a state of quiet or tranquility; a freedom from disturbance or agitation; harmony and concord.

There is also a definition which would have greater
identity and application to matters of public concern
generally, such as freedom from war; a cessation of hostilities; public quiet and tranquility; order and security,
such as is guaranteed by law; as, to keep the peace.

There is the further definition which seems to have a
more personal meaning and application to the individual
such as: Freedom from mental agitation or disturbance,
as from fear, terror, anger, anxiety, or the like; quietness
of mind; tranquility; calmness, spiritual calm or repose.

These definitions describe well *conditions* of "peace"
men seek to attain, individually and collectively; and, to
that end, they are helpful. But they do not explain the
way to reach, or to go about reaching, the results they
define.

Throughout the teachings of Jesus, as with this one He
now gives us to give to you, there always is presented in
one form or another the precept concerning the need of
each one to look to the Christ Light, the Divine Love,
which lies at and within the heart center of each one of
you. This mandate is ever present and is there to be
discovered by every one who looks carefully to what is being given. It is as a golden thread woven subtly into a
multicolored fabric, hidden from the undiscerning, yet
seen by those who truly endeavor to see, to know and to
understand these things.

We would suggest, dear brethren, that this is exactly
the situation presented here. This is the *Source* of the
peace to which Jesus speaks. The soul which seeks after
and gives obedience to the Will of the Father-Mother
God is placed upon the Path of Light. And it soon
discovers that should it follow, as best it can, the Way
shown by Jesus, the Christ Spirit within it begins to unfold and become an ever-present and functioning influence and force for good in its life. Slowly, the unfoldment continues, and, in time, there comes about a
greater understanding and recognition of the need for

continued obedience to Divine Law. This brings an even greater understanding of the *reality* of the Christ Light and the Love that it is. Thus there is brought to the soul the *reality* of peace. Profound in truth are the words of the psalmist: "Great peace have they which love Thy law."

Yet, there is prevalent among men the mistaken thought and belief that the criterion for peace is that relationship and condition wherein there are no open hostilities existent, especially as between countries and nations. A cessation of hostilities between countries which have been in conflict is indeed a step in the right direction, and one which all people should strive for. But this alone is not sufficient to meet the criterion or definition of peace as intended in these words of the Master.

Wherever there is disharmony, there is no true peace. We believe you will agree that a frank evaluation of the relationships which today exist upon your planet between many countries reveal that while there are few open hostilities, there, nevertheless, exists much distrust and disharmony between them. Perhaps it is the fear of a totally destructive atomic war which remains as the sole reason for an avoidance of open warfare.

Such relationships may be free from open conflict and the tragedy of war, however, they are not relationships tending to invoke the Laws of Brotherhood. They never give a lasting peace. Under such conditions, there constantly are currents of disharmony flowing between their leaders which tend to create a growing negative influence that could lead to open conflict; perhaps of even greater degree than what may have earlier prevailed.

We have used this example as one existing between nations, but what is being said applies equally to the relationships between men and races of men. Indeed, as we have set forth in an earlier message in The New Angelus, conflicts between nations and their governments, and between races of men, all have their beginning in individual thought and activity, and are able to gain and maintain their strength and vitality only through the efforts of individuals and groups of individuals.

Every government on your planet is composed of human beings whose combined wills make and assert the policies they express, and which generally are approved by the majority of the people they represent. There are exceptions to this statement, of course, but, in most instances, it is found that the responsibility for a country's actions can be traced back to its people; especially in those countries which have waged war against others.

Recently your own country was involved in a war in Viet Nam. Many of you prayed that this conflict would soon end, for it continued to build much adverse karma for your nation. It was meaningful that the people of your country were becoming more concerned about this, and it was good that greater urging and insistence was coming from the people that this conflict be terminated.

Man prays for peace. Man longs for peace, and, in great measure, strives for it. But, more often than not, his efforts are motivated by a desire to obtain every concession possible from his adversary. To put it another way, the dialogue may just as well be, "I seek peace with you, but upon *my* terms." The influence of the material world, and the corresponding influences of the humanistic element of his being, have rendered it difficult for man to realize and to understand that such a concern for self is what has gotten him into his predicament in the first place. And it is this wall of illusory belief, and the persuasions flowing from it, that must be penetrated and overcome. When they are, man will come to that place where he can finally work to bring about the peace, the true lasting peace he seeks. For then he will have learned that he must live in accordance with the guidance which truly comes from within—that truth which flows from the inner Higher Self.

The key to peace, to lasting peace, is love made manifest by man bringing forth the love, the Divine Presence within himself and letting this be the governing force of his life. It is willed and ordained by our Father-Mother God that this is to be the action of all men.

And so it is, that for there to be *real peace* among all men and nations, love must be fully manifested in the life of every one at all times. When love and brotherhood of man is the rule, rather than the exception, there shall indeed be "peace on earth and good will to all men."

But there are many who say that these conditions can never come to the planet Earth, and the thoughts and the hopes you may have for this to come to pass are but foolish dreams. To such persons we would simply say: God is love, and all He has created and continues to create is a creation and expression of His love. Thus, each of you is a product and a part of His love. And, being of this Divine Quality, ultimately the true nature of your being must become manifest and expressed in your life. This is true of every soul. So, it is only a matter of time within which your spiritual essence may unfold itself that this ultimate worldwide peace must become a reality. The only thing which has, so far, stood in the way of this coming about has been the exercise by man of his free will contrary to the Father's will.

Another factor which does much to bring despair and destroy the hopes of many for total peace is for the people to look upon this as an insurmountable task; that it is impossible to literally bring millions of people around to consciously seek after this purpose, when there is so much selfishness, greed, hate and resentment to be overcome. Obviously, the longer one continues to hang on to this point of view, the more his hope shall be lessened and weakened. But this is the negative approach. This is the view of the defeatist, who is content to remain in the darkness which only "the world gives." On the other hand, "Seekers after Light and Truth" know that such a state cannot always be, and they pursue the course their "spiritual self" opens to them that may lead them, and their brethren, into the peace that dwells in the Love of God.

Dearly beloved, this world and its inhabitants were not created in a single day, nor shall the peace of which we speak come about in a single day. But this goal shall surely be attained. This shall only come to be the reality it is destined to be through the process of evolution. It shall evolve much as the soul of man evolves. This may seem to many to be a very slow and tedious method, however, it is well for everyone to remember that this, too, is an outworking of God's Law and thus is sure and true in its ultimate result.

Frequently, we have sought to impress upon you the magnitude of the creative power you possess—the power of the mind; and of your need to guard carefully the use you make of it. We will not repeat what we have earlier said on this, only to say this: Each thought you send forth, dear ones, is a release of a force of energy out into the ethers of the universe which has the power to create whatever it encompasses, good or bad. The thought need not be expressed as a word or deed to be effective as an issued thought; silent or secret thoughts are indeed things of substance and of the power you give them.

Similarly, prayers are an important and a powerful force. A prayer issued forth in selfless love of God and fellow man, serves to do much good for all mankind. You have observed how the light of one small candle dispels completely the darkness into which it is placed. So, too, does one small prayer dispel the darkness toward which it is directed. And each thought of goodness is an active influence for good, joining with all others of like nature and purpose.

Most of you have at one time or another sought to "link in" your prayers with the prayers of other individuals and groups; thus to add strength both to your prayers and to those with whom you have "linked in." We would assure you that great power comes from this. "Like attracts like" has special meaning and application in this instance, as the function of this principle has consciously been invoked.

That you may better understand, we point out that each time you seek consciously to lend yourself and the power of your prayers to the prayers of others, you bring about this "linking in" which, in turn, triggers the phenomenon by which each prayer is substantially enhanced in its power, light and effect. As you may suppose, distance has no adverse affect upon the effectiveness of this process. Indeed, the prayers and thoughts expressed in this fashion prove to be very effective.

When the power of the mind is employed in this manner it receives the same benefits of enhancement. Indeed, this is the one part of your being whereby you may effectively serve as the instrument through which the power and strength of the God Presence you represent may be expressed for the good of every one. Thus you are able to render much help to others through this contact upon the level of the "invisible planes"; and even though they may be removed great distances from you.

Perhaps it becomes clearer to you that world peace need not appear as an insurmountable goal. For each effort you make in that direction, using the practices and techniques we have discussed, brings every one that much closer to this goal. It is extremely important that you, and all your brethren, realize that each such effort adds to the total effort and brings total world peace that much nearer to reality; and it is not a fruitless exercise in futility, as so many are wont to believe. Likewise, each act of kindness and brotherhood brings all of mankind a step nearer to the true relationship of brotherhood and peace. No single effort extended for this purpose, especially, is ever wasted or lost. Remember this!

Moreover, to each of you who participates in these actions of love, there comes an inner joy and peace, a feeling of real worth and belonging, an inner sense of knowing that this is in partial fulfillment, at least, of your real purpose in life. Added significance flows from the assurance that you are indeed a Child of God, a son and an heir, "a joint heir with the Christ our Lord."

As you permit the "Christ within" to control more and more your thoughts and motives, you experience a corresponding increase in power to do those things which are meant to be for the good of mankind. This, necessarily, adds to the sense of peace which this gives to you and to all who open themselves to it. And, of course, your ability to cope with earthly problems and to transmute evil into good is continuously improved. A paradox, perhaps, but true: As you serve one another, you serve God also, for you have brought God's Will into direct manifestation as your will; and there can be no finer step than this towards gaining for yourself and all your fellow men the reality of "heaven upon earth." And so may it be.

Chapter 5

LOVE—THE LAW OF BROTHERHOOD

Love One Another, As I have Loved You
(John 15:12)

GOD is Love. So spoke the Apostles, and so do we, time and time again, with thought and word centered upon this essential and fundamental truth.

Man, in his struggles of every day life upon the planet Earth, gives pause to question the truth that God is Love. Often there comes the negative and the disconcerting thought, "If God is Love, why must so much misfortune befall me? Why must I suffer so? Why must my loved ones face trial, suffering and travail in every form? Why is there so much poverty and inequality among men?"

And if man had only the ways and substance of the physical world to look to, and to rely upon, and only the manifestations which come through the actions of men, then, indeed, he would have cause to say, "If God is Love, then where is God?" For there would be little evidence of love to be found in such seeming tragedies.

But truth, dear ones, reaches far beneath the surface of things and the illusions which manifest to the physical eyes and physical senses of man. With even the slightest insight into truth, there begins to break through, perhaps ever so slightly at first, much as the first dim ray of sunlight at the breaking of dawn, the realization that all things which come into the life of man are nonetheless because of God's Love; that those events which seem so tragic are not punishment from God at all, but are the fruits of man's own doing; that man brings his suffering onto himself through disobedience of God's law and the misuse of the powers God has entrusted to him.

While it is true that God's law permits this, or operates in such a way that this occurs, man ultimately learns from these experiences that it is the fulfillment of Divine law which brings to him the realization that all is love; that because of the power of love, all adversity is overcome and replaced with that which is equal, just, good, kind and beautiful.

You shall come to understand and to know that God's love is with you, indeed, is the substance of your being. Thus do you seek to manifest your true nature, for this, too, is an attribute of your nature and of your purpose.

We give you our love always. As even now we touch you and you are blessed by and through the Grace of the Father, as we make above you the Sign of the Cross and cover you with His Light. We encourage you, dear ones, to remain steadfast in your endeavor to live and be the spiritual beings you truly are. We know the sorrows you have experienced. We know the difficulties you face, however, we also know that you have within you all the power and strength necessary to overcome and meet and cope with these problems. But it is for you to learn to use these powers which are within you; for they, too, are a gift of the Father of His love with which you are eternally endowed.

The Father's love blesses you, and, in the light that it places both within you and about you, there is to be found the abundant grace and the many powers it gives unto you and to all your fellow men. And it is meant for you to find these blessings, to know of them, to have them, and to have them more abundantly.

But there is an aspect of this gift of love which must be brought into expression that its grace may reach the fulfillment and completeness in your life which it is intended to have.

Now, while the Father gives all things so abundantly unto you and to all men, and for all time, there must come from each of you a response to what has been given you. Indeed, a response is necessary that there may come into fruition in your life the fulfillment and completeness intended.

You parents have given greatly of your love to your children. In various aspects, perhaps, but always in love have you given of yourselves to your children that their lives may be blessed and be made as complete as possible.

Think back to what feelings you experienced if no response came from them, when you received no reaction from them, one way or the other. Sometimes, perhaps, they refused to receive your love, or, at least, rejected it in part. And, if there were not any of these situations, there may have been occasions when they took what you gave them but abused it, or misused you and what you sought to give to them.

In any event, we dare say that there were occasions when you became quite provoked with your children because of their refusal to receive your love and kindness, or because of their lack of respect and appreciation for what you had given them.

On the other hand, there were the joyful experiences when they responded beautifully and it was no task at all to understand and to realize that they had truly and gratefully received of your love, and, in turn, were giving their love back to you and on to others. Thus the act of giving had become complete, for it had run its intended course and, in the process, blessed every soul it had reached.

Now we take this principle a step further and ask you to make a comparison between these earthly relationships with the relationship you have with your heavenly Father. Perhaps you should ask yourself the question:

"Have I responded to the Father's love He gives so graciously and so abundantly to me? Or have I neglected it, rejected it, or abused or misused it?"

You may find it necessary to answer in the affirmative to parts or all of this question, if you are fully honest with yourself. Yet, we know that this relationship has not all been negative. To the contrary, there has been an increasingly beautiful response flowing from you to the Father and to your fellow man.

We have asked you to make this comparison, not as a means of criticism, but, rather, as a way of demonstrating a means of gaining greater insight into yourself. And, as you do this, you must recognize even more fully how magnificently great is the Father's love.

For instance, another question: "Has the Father lessened His love any? Even when His children have failed to respond to it?" Absolutely not! Whereas, the human parent may find the strength of his love waning appreciably under such circumstances.

There is room for another comparison; this one between the reactions of the parent as compared to that of the Father. Again, an example by way of a question: "Did you find yourself disciplining your offspring because of their negative response to your offerings of love and kindness?" In all likelihood, you exercised some form of discipline.

But what has been the Father's reaction in this regard? Perhaps your initial thought was something like, "Yes, I was disciplined by the Father for my disobedience." However, we remind you that the discipline you may have been given was not given directly by the Father at all, but was the result of the outworking of that aspect of Divine law set into motion by your own earlier actions.

There may be some who would argue that if such discipline flows from Divine law, then, necessarily, it flows from the Father because He established this law. If this is the correct premise, then it must also follow that the discipline nevertheless is the result of the great love the Father has and holds for you in the first instance. It must always be kept in mind that *everything* flowing from God, *everything* He has created, has been because of—indeed, is a part of—His love. Therefore, His laws and their functions are so endowed and empowered. His law treats every one equally, fairly and justly, and has been so established that only the principle of love ultimately shall prevail among all His creation. Indeed, every aspect of Divine or Cosmic law is founded upon and sustained by the principle of love. Obviously, everything affected by these processes is treated in respect of that quality and character.

The fulfillment of Divine law may require imposition of karmic effects necessarily flowing from the causes which have set those effects into motion, for these are but a form of the dynamic nature of this principle. And, ultimately, these processes of purification shall effectively bring forth a manifestation of this very principle from the hearts which earlier rejected it.

And so you find that the Father has not failed at all to give you His love, nor has He lessened its flow to you whatsoever, because of anything you have done. Nor shall He ever do this, whether you have rejected His love, misused the powers he has given you, or directly disobeyed His will and His laws. Indeed, you shall find that the time shall come when in the very wake of the force of this phenomenon and power of God's love, the realization shall come to you of how beautifully true all this is and a tremendous and triumphant response shall well up from within your own heart and literally explode out into the universe in love and appreciation of all you have, and have received.

Yes, God is love. And if God is love, so too, are *you* love. For you are of God, created by Him and brought into life everlasting to serve as a channel through which He may give expression of His Presence, His power and His grace.

If the Father, in His love, is always so gracious and giving in His relationship with you, would it not be wise for you to follow after that example and strive more fully to become more giving in your relationships with others?

As you make sincere effort to do this, you shall immediately see manifestations of the truth which this is meant to bring to you. Of course, it is no easy task to grow into and achieve such an understanding relationship with all your fellow men. But it is a task and a goal you have set before yourself, and upon which you have embarked.

It is indeed a blessing to receive of the Father's love, just as it is a profound blessing to give freely and fully of it unto others. Indeed, this is one of the great mysteries of the power of Divine Love.

Meditate upon our words, dearly beloved brethren, take them into your hearts, and give them life. Let these principles become your actions. Give them expression and you shall find that God is speaking through you, and to you as well.

MEDITATION — A CONTEMPLATION

We would have you still your minds, quiet your hearts, and open yourselves to the beautiful light of your countenance: The Light which dwells within, the Christ.

To assist you in carrying this out, we would suggest you use the powers of your mind to envision the scene we describe.

Picture yourself seated upon the shore of a very beautiful lake. The ground is cushioned by a heavy growth of beautiful dark green grass, vibrant both in color and to your touch.

There are tall mountains all about, their peaks covered with glistening snow. The air is crystal clear, fresh and exhilarating. You inhale deeply its lifegiving and invigorating substance, breathing in the beautiful power and life that it gives.

There are trees completely surrounding the lake. They are tall and stately, standing as majestic sentinels, guarding and protecting all the beauty of this glorious panorama of the Father's creation unfolded before you. And all this beauty your eyes behold is canopied by a magnificently brilliant blue, cloudless sky.

In this environment of heavenly endowed beauty, you quickly find that you have easily divorced yourself from your worldly cares and concerns as you gaze upon and contemplate the beauty and the grace of the Father's handiwork.

The surface of the lake is absolutely still, not a single ripple appears. It is as a huge mirror, reflecting clearly and precisely the trees, the mountains, the sky. And, as you look to this reflection, you see that a perfect likeness of your own image is also reflected from the water's surface which, after a time, melds into and becomes a part of the total reflection—it is as if all things have become one.

Then, suddenly, as if an invisible being or force had moved upon the surface of the water, ripples and waves have formed upon the surface. And, as this disturbance increases, the beautiful reflections become more and more distorted and now it becomes difficult to make out the form and shape of the objects reflected. Although the objects in the reflection are now poorly defined and distorted, you know that they are still actually present and in their proper form.

As you contemplate this experience, the realization should become clear that you have had demonstrated for you a condition that exists within you. Every truth you

have learned and experienced, every understanding you
have gained, every new realization and increase in
awareness has become a part of and remains within your
consciousness. And, being a part of your consciousness,
they are a part of *you;* for you are consciousness.

But do the disturbances and upsets of the daily life,
and the problems they may present, whether large or
small, ruffle and disturb you and your actions? Do these
disturbances have the power to create a distortion of
what you may manifest outwardly? Or, do you realize
that what happens outside yourself, and around you, are
happenings upon the surface of life and need not affect
what lies within you, your real Self. Thus, you may judge
as to whether you allow yourself to become controlled by
forces lying outside yourself rather than by the powers of
your true Inner Self—the "Father within."

Recall the beautiful reflection of the "still waters" and
place yourself solely within the influence of the magnificent light and power of the Father's love with which you
are eternally blessed. For you shall immediately sense a
resurgence of His power within you and find the
strength, wisdom and power to cope with whatever problems there may be.

Chapter 6

SPIRITUAL EVOLUTION

All the Father's creation is and has being forever-more and the manifestation of its being will pass through various phases and aspects as it unfolds and fulfills its purpose as outlined by divine plan.

SPIRITUAL evolution is dynamic and occurs simultaneously both within your inner being and in the world surrounding you. It is for you to discern these changes and to be aware of their impact that you may understand that all change occurs ultimately to produce good.

You have noticed changes occurring in your lives; not only in your growing knowledge, scientifically and otherwise, and in the physical things with which you may be concerned, but also in relationships between men, from the standpoint of both their business and social activities. Perhaps even more significantly, you witness an almost spectacular change occurring in the areas having to do with religious and spiritual matters.

None of these areas are really separated from one another. While each has its immediate area of influence and effect, there is an interaction and an interrelation occurring and existing in all relationships, as in all aspects of life, on your plane and on ours; indeed, upon all planes.

In all areas, however, there are new levels of acceptance of that which is bad and evil. For example, you see

45

a marked decline in moral standards in social and personal relationships and also in business affairs and ethics. The trust that one person may place in another, which, for a long time, was a matter of pride and respect in the business affairs of men in your nation, has been lost to many. It was not too long ago—in the sense of time, as you know it to be—when a person's word was his bond. While there are still many who are worthy of this trust, this is no longer true in most instances.

In organized religions and in independent spiritual movements, as well, there is literally, in many areas of the world, an outcropping of new approaches to various philosophies and the development of many new movements and cults, some of which seem to be fixing new and higher goals of attainment for their followers and memberships. The fact that man would be concerned with reaching higher goals and levels of consciousness and awareness would seem to be a matter for rejoicing, but, alas, far too many of these undertakings seek primarily to commercialize upon man's desire to "awaken and seek" after higher ideals and values. Indeed, many advocate and teach only techniques for more rapid psychic development, and employ practices which hasten the opening of the individual's psychic centers, without any apparent regard to true spiritual unfoldment and attainment. Thus, many are exposed to substantial danger of emotional damage and disorders.

There is much travail. The growing evil influence of the anti-Christ becomes more apparent during this period of transition into the New Age.

As we speak in this vein, dear ones, we do not mean to tell you that the New Age shall "arrive" tomorrow, or the day after that, or in the next year or so. The transition from one Age into the next is a gradual process which is already underway. Exactly when this shall be completed should be of no concern to you at this moment. Indeed, the paramount concern of each of you should be with what you may do with your lives "today" to better cope with your daily needs and to better equip yourself to take from the good things of life.

Recently, we reminded the readers of The New Angelus of this important truth: All things evil are in time transmuted into things good. In your own lives, you do not destroy the evil within yourself, you learn to overcome it. The energy you use for evil can just as well be used for good. Indeed, all things come from God and are good; it is the use to which they are put by men, that makes them evil. And it is only the process of change in man's motives, desires and purposes that bring about change in the nature of the actions flowing from him.

As above, so below. As in the universe, so within you. As within, so without. That which you see in others, dwells also within you. Thus, you shall come to more readily understand that that which bespeaks evil also heralds the coming of good. But the hearts of men must change for this to come about to the degree that it is meant to be. God has willed all things to be good. Now it must be man's will that this shall be so. Strive therefore to bring goodness into all realms of life.

Indeed, dearly beloved, the blessings of life are numberless. The greatness of life far exceeds your fondest dreams. Happiness in life is not a myth or fantasy, it is meant to be a reality of life for each of you; for, indeed, it is a reality. It is a product of God's love. And, remember, so are you!

We recognize the feelings you have in your hearts, and the disappointments that have come to you over the recent years because of the ending of relationships and the passing away of certain things. We have taught upon this at other times and shall not now dwell upon this, except to say: Unless the old does pass away, the new cannot come into being.

This is a process of life. Life is dynamic in its very being and essence. And that which is dynamic is ever-changing. Look to your own lives. You need but to look back over only a short span of time, perhaps, to find that there has been much change in your thinking, in your desires, purposes, concepts and ideas. And, as you continue upon this, your chosen path, you shall continue to experience such changes in yourself. Indeed, pray that such changes shall continue; strive for it that there may be provided this means for spiritual growth and the unfoldment of your divine nature.

Change is a beautiful process in its own right. There are times when you may undergo what seems to be a very traumatic experience, only to find later — when able to look back upon it more objectively — that what actually occurred was the outworking of God's law; and in such way as to be the most beneficial and helpful result possible.

This, beloved brethren, is universal law in action. It works in your life and in the lives of all others; indeed, throughout all creation. There is no stopping change, it shall always be an active occurrence of life.

Taking charge of the changes occurring within the inner self, you are often unaware of how the same evolution is occurring in the world around you. Have you recently looked to the far horizon, or even beyond to the farthest reaches of your vision, and sought to take in and to behold the beauty of all you could see? Indeed, we would suggest that you give pause to this thought, to the extent that if you do not have opportunity to do so this evening, then, do this the first thing tomorrow morning.

Look out upon the creation in which you dwell, look to the farthest point of your vision and make special effort to look beyond the activities and the scenes to which you have become so accustomed and learned to expect in your daily pursuits. Look for the real majesty and beauty of the Father's creation within your environment.

So much has been said about the planet Earth as a school of life which serves as a "school of hard knocks" —

to borrow a contemporary expression — and correctly so, for life upon this planet is indeed fraught with tribulation and difficulty. It is much as going from mountain to valley and valley to mountain, up and down, from cycle to cycle, end on end.

And as you concentrate upon this aspect of life on Earth, there is a tendency to develop the attitude that this planet is an ugly place to live. So much so, perhaps, that you may come to despise it and to think of it only as a place from which you would wish to leave, if given the opportunity to do so.

But this beloved planet is not of that dimension at all. Gross forms of life are manifested upon this plane, as indeed there must be, but beautiful experiences and manifestations of the Father's creation are also a part of this plane.

You have a saying: "Beauty is in the eye of the beholder." This is indeed an expression of truth. For it is always how you view an object, a circumstance, or condition in your life that determines the impression it makes upon you.

Perhaps you wonder why we would concentrate upon this theme. We do so lest you would forget that you have been placed into a plane of life and an environment which is designed to teach you to look for and to see the beauty that is in all the forms of life expressed about you; that you would learn to realize that beauty is manifested in every form of creation.

This is also an important experience because this practice and exercise in observation and discernment furnishes an excellent background for developing a positive attitude and point of view rather than a negative one. Indeed, the habit that man unfortunately seems so prone to follow, of concentrating far too much energy and thought upon negative attitudes and points of view, rather than upon positive, beautiful and meaningful ones, fits very well into this aspect of this principle.

Although there may be arguments to the contrary, the truth remains that sooner or later man expresses externally that which he holds within his heart. Therefore, if you find yourself expressing only thoughts, ideas and attitudes which are negative then you should hasten to take an inventory of what you harbor within, and examine carefully the principles and purposes you are holding to that are allowing you to form such negative patterns. This is so necessary, for your outer expressions are indeed the expression of what is flowing from your heart.

On the other hand, and far more importantly, if the converse is true, that is, the attitudes, principles and purposes motivated by the inner self are of a positive nature, then, beloved brethren, you find that that which flows into and through your life is indeed beautiful and spiritually uplifting.

It is not at all a foolish fantasy or dream to look for the beautiful things in life. Nor is it a facade to consciously place beautiful thoughts and ideas where there have been none before. For beautiful things are brought into being by such form of positive endeavor and are given the incentive to manifest and to demonstrate that power and that quality.

This, too, beloved brethren, is a purpose of your life. You seek in this life incarnate to better learn to express, to give, to create and to foster that which is beautiful and which can be made beautiful. No simple task this. Indeed, were it not difficult, you would not have accepted it as an assignment of responsibility for this incarnation. You seek to perform tasks and to reach goals which are difficult and thus you gain in strength and increase the flow of the Christ light and the God Presence which is within you.

There are many forms and means by which one may give expression to those things which are beautiful. The various forms of art provide a means for man to express his creative and artistic gifts and power. These are the more apparent forms utilized. But there is yet another means that has to do with perfecting the relationships which exist between you and your neighbor — your fellow man.

Are the attitudes and views you hold towards your fellow man worthy of this classification? If not, then why not? For the power is within you to develop those positive and helpful views and attitudes, and change them as may be necessary, to bring about and to produce a beautiful relationship. And so long as you delay or postpone doing anything about this, you effectively prevent it from becoming a beautiful one, as it should be.

If you answer, "It is not I who is responsible for our negative relationship; it is because of *his* attitudes and *his* views towards me, that such a relationship exists!" to this response, we simply say: If this is what you truly think and believe, it is still your responsibility to help your brother bring about any changes that may be needed in his thinking by maintaining within yourself constantly the positive nature and character we have suggested. Do not, however, busy yourself with trying to change him directly, for you shall find these attempts both unsuccessful and disruptive of your relationship. Rather, you do this exclusively through the example you set for him by practicing these principles as best you can, by your thoughts and prayers in his behalf. As you follow this practice, you shall, in due time, observe changes in his attitudes towards you for the betterment of your relationship.

Yes, all things in your life may be made beautiful if you try to make them so. And it matters not that there may be those about you who would rather tear down or seek to make ugly your efforts for good. It is what you give to this effort that counts and really matters in your life and in your relationships with your fellow man and with God.

The life that is yours, as with all life, is indeed a beautiful gift from God, our Father-Mother. Take this gift and use it in such a way as to reap the bountiful harvest of blessings which flow always from the Father's love. And it is His Love with which we bless you now and give to you as abundantly as we possibly can, for this is as it has been given unto us.

As it has been said so many times before by all teachers, and as by the beloved Master Jesus: You must have the faith to know that God is indeed with you and within you; and when you call upon Him, you invoke the power of His Love to bring forth the good which is intended.

When your actions are motivated by a desire to bring goodness and well-being into the lives of your fellow man, you are motivated by the God Presence within. Indeed, you thus serve as a means by which God can do His work upon Earth.

We would speak for a moment upon recent prophecies which have predicted that catastrophic and destructive forces are to strike many nations.

There are several factors which you must always take into consideration when evaluating such predictions. First, the precognition or visions that are received by those gifted to receive them are, nevertheless, being received by a human being, and, being human, they are not perfect. Frequently, but not always, what is thus perceived by them upon the invisible planes may be misinterpreted or misunderstood. They may fail to relate it in its proper significance, or it may be influenced somewhat by the character and the background of the individual receiving them. This is not intentional, but by its very nature, this is a problem associated with this form of acitivity. Indeed, every sincere and dedicated channel or prophet recognizes that these conditions exist and must be contended with.

Secondly, assuming that the prediction as related is an accurate description of what has been perceived upon the invisible planes, it must be remembered that these relate existing tendencies and not necessarily one's destiny or fate. For there is ever present the power of free will and freedom of choice. Remember, beloved brethren, what has been said concerning this power that is held by each individual soul. Even the Father will not interfere with the exercise of that power.

Therefore, any predictions relating to individuals are necessarily subject to what power and influence of change may be wrought through the exercise of their free will. Indeed, such tendencies may well be changed, altered, or perhaps even blocked completely.

This also in great measure applies to predictions relating to various phenomena of nature. You should recognize the need to avoid any attitude and feeling of fear or insecurity, and to control your reactions to these things that your thoughts and expectations may continue to be of a positive nature. What has been said concerning the power of prayer certainly applies to these matters as well.

A genuine sense of well-being, of safety, of being "truly held in the hands of God," regardless of the circumstances or events, may always be your strength when you invoke the power of God's Presence and Love as an active force in your life.

We would suggest you turn the pages of your Bible to the Old Testament and study the story of Sodom and Gomorrah for the assurance given there that "I will not destroy it for ten's sake" is as valid today as it was then. Indeed, "Put on the whole armor of God that you may be able to stand against" all that would harm you. We would urge you to practice these principles and thus allow yourself to be counted as being among the righteous and gain the fruits that such righteousness brings.

And finally, by all means continue in your prayers for peace. For you have witnessed, and shall continue to witness, the power of prayer being made manifest in the minds and hearts of men who but a short time ago spoke only of war. Oh yes, there are yet many who would prefer war, and who would profit materially because of their greed and their individual desire for material gain through this means. But these individuals do not need to have their way, and their desires do not need to be fulfilled. Use the powers the Father has entrusted to you and pray that only truth and the peace it brings shall prevail.

Before we leave the discussion on change, however, it is well that we touch on the one single thing which most frequently impedes or stands in the way of spiritual evolution. Fear and the aspect of fear which has to do with the "fear of failure" can very often slow your progress.

Each of you has had trouble with this state of mind from time to time, and it has been a substantial obstacle to you. This has also been the case with most of your brethren, if not all of them.

For a moment, think back to what happened on many occasions when you wished very much to do something you felt would have been of considerable interest and value to your life. You likely recall that, as you neared the point of taking some action in that regard, your mind became filled with thoughts of fear of failure and many doubts began to take over. And, as you let this state of mind grow and flourish, the decision was made to postpone and delay launching into this new project or endeavor for the time being. Thus you lost the benefits you could have gained from having taken this step; and, most likely, later experienced regret and disappointment in yourself for not having followed your initial guidance.

This kind of episode and experience should be guarded against, especially in your spiritual interests. This is not to say that you are to disregard common sense and sound reasoning, but it is to say that you must heed carefully your intuition and inner guidance.

Your endeavors after spiritual growth and increased awareness are never failures, regardless of the immediate results. Even those times when you find yourself moving along a path which you conclude is the wrong path for you, are not failures. True enough, such experiences bring disappointments and appear to be failures and losses, but they are not.

Indeed, each such experience has brought you an experience from which you may gain greatly in knowledge and wisdom. For this has been an experience in living and not just one of an intellectual nature.

You need not go back very far in this lifetime to find occasions when you suffered disappointment. You felt then that your actions had resulted in failure for the results you expected did not come into fruition. But later, when you were in a position to be more objective about it, you were able to see that you had profited from the experience.

Frequently, in fact, experiences of this nature are of a far greater value to your overall growth than they would have been had your project initially reached the success intended for it. It is somewhat of a paradox, but the mind remembers much better and much more clearly the experiences which were fraught with difficulty and failure than those which were easily passed through. Ultimately you shall come to the realization that the greater portion of your present level of awareness and consciousness has most likely been gained from your "failures" than from your "successes."

We would, therefore, suggest that when you sense thoughts and inner urgings to move into certain directions and to seek after new vistas and new understanding, you answer them by taking affirmative action in their behalf. Do not let indecisiveness or fear of failure stand in the way of action. Oh yes, practice discrimination and use your knowledge and your wisdom to choose the path you would follow, but do not allow the power of reason and logic to serve as an excuse to stand still.

Move forward, and if, after a time, you discover that your choice was not the best one, or that the course you have taken is the wrong one for you, do not stew in the negativity of unnecessary disappointment, self-pity and sorrow, or feel that your time has been wasted. Instead, quickly place yourself upon another path and pursue it.

You should see that your efforts have not been wasted at all. You have learned of something that you likely will not do again, or, perhaps, shall endeavor to repeat, but differently. In any event, this form of action, with a positive attitude, gives you an excellent outlook and approach to the many challenges of life.

And such is the power of Divine Love. It is creative and brings always with it its inherent restorative powers. When you consciously seek to include this as a part of your motivations and your attitudes, whatever the results, they shall carry with them the blessing which this love gives them. Thus, your activities may serve as beautiful expressions of this very same power.

These are also the actions of a "seeker after truth," a disciple of the Beloved Master, who follows his path of life eager to join with his brethren who are also seeking the beautiful Presence of the Father in all things.

Do not let the fear of failure, or any form or nature of fear, for that matter, stand in the way of your seeking after the fulfillment of your purposes in life. Do not let worry over whether or not you shall succeed or fail stand in the way of your endeavors.

Instead, hold always strong in the faith that the power of the Father is within you, blesses and guides you upon the path you tread. *Know* that you shall indeed succeed. But how far you shall move along your path depends upon you, for you are the one who must take the steps. And be they but one step at a time, nevertheless, they must be taken. Take them in confidence, for you are truly a Child of God. Thus you are endowed with all things of the Father—mightily, abundantly, and eternally—and they are your inheritance and your life.

Chapter 7

EXERCISES IN LOVE

SPIRITUAL advancement of the inner self does not occur on its own. We are pressed to take on responsible practices. Our mind accomplishes the outer understanding of the laws that govern our existence. Yet our hearts must put into practice these principles in order that we achieve true spiritual growth. Often, the simplest actions have the most noticeable effect, as when we start practicing the principles of humility, giving, and true service.

HUMILITY

When we explore the principle of humility, we are brought to the fact that Jesus placed great value by its practice.

It is no secret that Jesus sought to make clear by His teachings that the way to God's kingdom is not open to the proud, the haughty, the mighty, and the arrogant. Yet it seems that, next to patience, the virtue of humbleness of character and being is the most difficult for most persons to practice.

We think the importance of this is pointed up by the fact that the New Testament records this as having been spoken by Jesus no less than three times, and in much the same form a fourth time. These teachings also direct attention to the simple truth that this is a quality of self-control which must be willed by the individual. Each one must first desire to become and be of humble and unpretentious nature and bearing, and then follow practices which develop this virtue.

This also carries forward the truth appearing so frequently throughout the Christ's teachings: That each one owes to himself—and to God as well—the responsibility to strive after a constant willingness to turn to the Christ within, to the Essence of God which is there, that It may unfold and become increasingly manifested in his life. For until there is such willingness, there does not exist the genuineness of purpose and motive which must underlie these efforts to attain true humbleness of self.

The incentive for the willingness to seek after humbleness proceeds from your Higher Self. The desires and forces that would oppose its attainment originates within the lower mortal or worldly self. Herein lies the reason for the extreme difficulty you may encounter within yourself when you undertake to gain spiritual unfoldment and growth. With each effort you make to take a step forward on the path of spiritual truth and light, you always are confronted by one or more of the many negative elements of your lower nature which would deter or prevent your progress.

And so the conflict and struggle rages within. Moreover, this does not take into account the negative influences from external sources which also have their own part to play in all this. However, those which come from yourself are the main concern at the moment. It would be well, therefore, to remain aware of these two facets of your being and thus be in a better position to understand what is likely to occur in that regard.

When we categorize generally the qualities of the humble person we find one who is modest, meek, unpretentious, restrained, reserved, unostentatious, unselfish, kind and loving. On the other hand, when we look to the opposite quality of character, we find one who is proud, vain, conceited, egotistical, cocky, self-important, self-esteeming, self-admiring, puffed up, and self-exalting. Indeed, this latter class of persons may be more appropriately and simply described as being "totally selfish," for all these characteristics are, in some way, a form of selfishness. Whereas selflessness is the hallmark of the humble person, of one who gives of himself in love and in service because of his love for his fellow man, without thought of self.

As you consider the teachings of Jesus given in conjunction with this truth, you find well defined descriptions of character and behavior setting apart the humble and the meek from the proud and the selfish. Indeed, you find these repeated often.

We would stress the importance attached to your need to recognize and to work with your own shortcomings. Man seems to find it much easier to judge others, and to discern their faults, than to judge fairly his own faults. And to do this, he places himself above others through a falsely supported self-righteous belief; and this is a terrible mistake for him to make. There is much danger associated with any conduct that approaches, in any form, upon self-exaltation. With this, there necessarily are involved practices which adopt purposes for self alone, which usually prevent the development of any really good relationships with others.

For example: Do you engage in the practice of raising your own ego and self-esteem through criticism of others? Do you, when you speak of others, extol their good points, or are you quick to speak of what you consider to be their weaknesses? Do you engage in and help pass along gossip, or do you let it stop with you? Do you take delight in any mishap and difficulty which may befall a competitor, or others, or do you give them your help and assistance?

These questions are but a sampling of what may easily enter into one's thoughts and actions. These are the products of the lower self which still endeavors to control the mind and to allow these thoughts to prevail. It is this aspect of your thinking with which you are to be concerned. That is, what effort will you make to control the direction your thoughts, your desires and actions may take? What shall their final form be as they manifest and flow out from you into your external world? There exists within you the power to control this. Indeed, dear brethren, you have the power to choose whether they shall be along the path of love and selflessness, or along the path of darkness. Which path shall you choose?

To seek after the way of the humble is the answer. But the way is not easy upon the Earth plane. The powers of the lower self are strong, having fed upon the homage you have paid, unwittingly perhaps, to worldly desires over the long period of your existence. These ties are strong and are not easily severed or broken. But they must be, if true humble stature is to be attained. This is what has brought you to the inner conflict and struggle which rages even now between these two aspects of your being. The lower self does not wish to yield to the urgings and promptings of the Higher Self; indeed, it seeks to hold on with all the strength it can muster.

Attainment of an humble heart necessarily ends the reign of the lower nature of man. For then the power and the strength of the heart mind — the Christ mind — overpowers that which may come from the body mind, depriving the lower self of any channel through which it may manifest; thus, perhaps, to atrophy and die.

In humbleness there is strength. Indeed, within the recorded words of the Master Jesus, you find Him saying: "Whoever humbles himself like this child, he is the greatest in the kingdom of heaven. . . . Blessed are the poor in spirit (the humble), for theirs is the kingdom of heaven. . . . Blessed are the meek, for they shall inherit the earth. . . . Come unto me all who labor and are heavy laden, and I will give you rest. Take my yoke upon you, and learn of me; for I am meek and lowly in heart: and you shall find rest unto your souls."

This always has been the teaching of the Christ Spirit. So were the Apostles taught. Indeed, you find in the writings and teachings of both Peter and James: "God opposes the proud, but gives grace to the humble."

It follows that you must seek after the way of the humble and meek of heart, striving step by step after such quality of perfection. Although the way be difficult and narrow, it is, nevertheless, always open to you. And, sooner or later, each one realizes that he must undertake this journey.

To the proud and self-righteous there only comes in time humiliation, shame, indignity and suffering. For there is no escape from the immutable ultimate outworking of God's laws. Every man gathers the fruits of his deeds. Remember: "Whosoever shall exalt himself shall be abased; and he that shall humble himself shall be exalted."

We have spoken of the difficulty one may expect to encounter upon striving after attainment of the virtue of humbleness, yet we hasten to add that you not be forlorn or apprehensive about your success. Indeed, avoid at all costs any fear of failure. Bring into your consciousness the strength which is already yours. Use the power of the love within you which seeks always to be released from the center of your being that it may do its good works.

O, dearly beloved, do not dwell upon that which may bring harm and darkness. Rather, concentrate upon that which God has placed within you that you may have light, indeed, that you may *be* Light. Use this Presence, this power of Love, as a source of strength and courage to help you in your journey back to the Father, for this is of its intended purpose.

Your present duality of being — the Higher Self and the lower self, the positive and the negative aspects, the good and the evil — all serve to provide you with the means to grow spiritually. Indeed, you have witnessed in your own life — as with all levels of creation — that struggle, conflict and friction are the catalysts for evolvement and growth. It is for the Infinite Wisdom to have known of the beauty these experiences yield to the soul of man; that he may learn to use and to transmute the low, the negative and the evil into the Higher. Thus that purposes of evil may become instead manifestations of love.

While the door opening onto the way of the humble heart may be locked and difficult to open, there always is a key. The key is your earnest desire and *YOUR WIL- LINGNESS* to enter upon it. And as you remain willing — truly willing — to achieve that state of being, the way is opened ever wider and you are shown the steps you must take. Your guidance becomes more easily discerned and understood and the path ahead becomes better lighted and more easily followed. Some of the steps may remain difficult because of deep rooted character defects and shortcomings that need to be removed, but they become more meaningful and desirable of attainment and you gladly continue on to your goal.

And so it is that now you find yourself upon this path that leads towards ultimate perfection. Already you have discovered that this path is one with valleys and hills, with times of growth and times of dormancy, with times of joy and times of struggle. But whatever your stage of attainment, if there is present an awareness in both your heart and your mind that all that is, has been, or ever will be, comes into your life from God and because of His love; that you are indeed a child of God, destined to become perfect, as is the Christ perfect; and that you and all your brethren are held alike in God's love, then, do you really *KNOW* that all is well.

GIVING

We come to the task of practicing the principle of giving.

When the thought of giving is communicated to the human mind, immediately, to the minds of most, comes the thought that this means the giving of things, of material gifts. And, to the majority of persons, this form of giving is basically the only one to which much, if any, consideration is given.

While this form of giving is, no doubt, an essential and significant form for expressing this principle on the human plane, and plays an important role in meeting human needs, the principal thought we would seek to give you concerning this principle has to do with the *giving of self.*

You have heard it said: "The more you give, the more you shall receive." The Beloved Master Jesus taught this principle. It runs as a golden thread throughout all His teachings.

On the other hand, the more you hold onto your gifts and talents, and seek to keep them unto yourself, the more quickly and completely you shall lose them. As they are held back, and selfishly kept from expression, they become dormant; and the growth and unfoldment they are destined to produce is delayed, or even lost.

Frequently, we have stated to you who are members of Prayer Healing Groups, that when you meet together to give of your prayers for healing and to send forth your thoughts and prayers of love selflessly and with a deep and sincere purpose of giving of the Father's love unto the brethren for whom you pray, you are truly giving of yourself. When this occurs, there is always a corresponding but greater blessing flowing back to you. This is, in part, an outworking of the "law of flow."

When you send forth thoughts of kindness rather than thoughts of criticism, when you entertain thoughts and express words of praise and goodness for another rather than of gossip about them, when you pray for others and give them thoughts of encouragement and wishes for their success, even though their success may be in competition with your own, you follow well the principle of giving and obey its precepts.

To conform to this practice may require that you make substantial adjustments and changes in your thinking habits and actions. Old habits, ideas, and concepts contrary to this principle must yield to new ones supportive of it, if such changes are to occur.

You can take much encouragement, hope and enthusiasm from this fact: That you *are* making progress in changing your ways towards this more positive direction. Indeed, if you objectively view your behavior in this regard from the standpoint of what it was like in the past to what it is like now, you can see that you have already changed much in your life for the better. Obviously, you are interested in what you do with yourself, otherwise, you would not be studying this material and seeking after knowledge of the principles we discuss and teach.

There are those who would ask, "Why do you dwell upon these matters? Why are you not giving us greater insight into the deeper mysteries of life? Why do you not disclose to us more fully the secret teachings of the Ancient Wisdom, or of what lies ahead of us?"

And there are also those who would have us enter into studies and training which would assist them to more quickly reach matters lying substantially beyond their present level of understanding and consciousness, thus hoping to cut short and eliminate what may seem to them to be numerous and needless obstacles in their path.

To you, who would so question and who seek after shortcuts we would remind you: *There are no shortcuts* to the attainment of truth nor to gaining spiritual awareness and the evolvement and unfoldment of the spiritual Self. It is an absolute necessity that you learn to follow these principles, to the point of taking them into your lives and making them a part of your active daily living.

Until this becomes a reality for you, you cannnot gain the spiritual growth your soul requires.

God's plan requires an orderly development and evolution of His creation. You are a part of His plan. Therefore, it is essential that your evolution move forward in an orderly manner. We seek to help you do this with the teachings and guidance we give you. As you give obedience to the plan, which brings you under the disciplines that require your involvement with these principles, you become aware of the flow of the beautiful, beneficent fruitage of Divine Love.

For example, consider the parable of the prodigal son. You recall that the errant child of the parable did not first have to complete his return to his father's home before receiving of the father's love. Indeed, as the account says, "But when he was yet a great way off, his father saw him and had compassion, and ran, and fell on his neck, and kissed him."

Do you not gain from this teaching the significance it holds for you? This tells you exactly what occurs when you seek to return to the Father. Although you may be yet a long way off, the Father has come out to meet you. He has compassion for you and He blesses you and He takes you in His arms and kisses you, giving you abundantly of His love. Meditate upon this profoundly beautiful truth, dear brethren.

TRUE SERVICE

Following somewhat upon that vein, we would now discuss another important principle. In fact, we believe that your living according to this principle will do as much as anything else, if not more, to bring about the full manifestation of love in your life. This principle is the one of "Service."

An honest and persistent effort to improve and to grow spiritually, and thus unfold the beautiful, inherent essence and nature of the Christ which lies within, is perhaps the most important virtue for you to work towards. And this endeavor, to be of service to your fellow man, is a most effective and beneficent means of working towards that purpose. Indeed, as you serve your fellow man, you serve the Father. And, in such service, you ultimately learn of the value of the quality of selflessness; that this should be the keynote of all your endeavors.

This concept and aspect of selflessness and service, a complete surrender of the self, is the difficult task it is because its demands are so diverse from the demands of the material world in which you must presently live. The attitudes, concepts, and ideas which are attuned to the human, earthly life are always difficult to remove or replace. Yet, sooner or later, the change from all thinking and action which is of a selfish nature to that which is absolutely selfless must come about.

A most profound paradox indeed is the truth expressed by the Beloved Master when he said, "For whosoever will save his life shall lose it; and whosoever will lose his life for my sake shall find it." Thus, the more one seeks to hold onto the earthly life and the things of that life, the more he loses. Whereas, the more he gives of himself and surrenders of the self to his Higher Self, the more he gains of the true life.

It is said that "action is the magic word." Truly, service is action, positive action, which requires affirmative and loving effort. And this, dearly beloved brethren, is what you seek to fulfill in this life; a profoundly wise path indeed.

Much has been written and spoken upon this matter of "service," and, no doubt, much of what we say, we have said many times before. Nevertheless, the fact remains that man seems to have much difficulty learning that this function is essential to his spiritual well-being. Indeed, he learns that without it his spiritual growth suffers because of its being absent from his active purposes.

As you review the teachings and ministrations of the Master Jesus, you find that everything He said and did was, in one form or another, a service to mankind. In time, the realization shall come to you of what great value and virtue this form of action can bring to your life. Yet man seems reluctant to work towards this goal.

Perhaps the difficulty arises from his failure to understand just how broad and inclusive the scope and meaning of this principle is and can be. Frequently, when the subject of service is brought up for consideration or discussion, his first reaction is to think of it as being some form of physical help or action, or material aid to another. Generally, he tends to limit his idea of service as being solely of this nature or involving the performance of menial tasks and burdens for another person. While such conduct is, of course, included within the scope of the service to which we speak, it is not meant to be so limiting as that. Indeed, the ways and the means through which he may serve others are myriad. He need only to recognize the opportunities when presented, then accept the responsibilities they present as a part of his own and act upon them. These opportunities are the source of experiences for which his soul yearns and can gain in no other way.

There are in the minds of many questions of what this entails. What may they do to fulfill this responsibility? Although specific suggestions can be made, we would suggest that the words of the Master give an appropriate and adequate answer, wherein He says, "If any one serves me, he must follow me. . . . I am the way, the truth, and the life." So, if you would endeavor to become more Christlike, and thus "follow" Him, you must follow after His "way" of life.

This places before you a clearly discernible definition of what is needed from you to carry out this principle. This makes it simpler for you to understand what is expected of you. To live such a life, it is necessary that you make conscious effort daily to follow the guidelines the Master has set before you. Through His life, He has portrayed for you what your life is to be, and shall be.

Thus you learn to bring good into the lives of others. "By their good works shall you know them." By your good works shall you be known!

We shall discuss some of the areas in which you may pursue this purpose. But, first, we discuss an important aspect which must be considered in relation to the matter of service. This has to do with your motives. What are the motivations prompting you to enter into this purpose?

Perhaps the best way to understand its importance is to examine some of your own experiences. For instance, what have been your reactions when someone has treated you with kindness? Have you wondered about *their* motives? Perhaps with thoughts that may have gone something like this: "I wonder what they are up to? What do they want from me?" Have your thoughts been colored by such scepticism?

If so, then you must recognize your feelings and attitudes as being the product of the selfishness which persists in the practices, customs and thinking of the public generally and the influence of the material and worldly concepts of the life in which you must presently live. The ever present quest after material wealth and power adds to the strength of this malignancy. Greed eats away at every precept which supports and commands integrity, honesty and decency as a part of man's day to day relationships. It also feeds off the weaknesses of the lower self of his being, enabling him to yield to the drives of the human ego for self-exaltation and selfishness in every form.

You find yourself literally surrounded by the influence of the negative worldly forces that oppose all that is good, all that is godly. Similarly, you are confronted with the negative aspects of your own lower self, and their insidious nature. We, therefore, stress the need for you always to examine carefully into your own motives as you enter into active pursuit of the purpose under discussion. For it is here, at this level of thinking and fixing of desire, that you govern the direction in which you choose to move and establish your purpose. It is here that you select the paths you will follow. Indeed, it is here that you determine whether you shall be selfless or selfish.

Your motives are the fruitage of what is in your heart; this is their source. Until they are in some way made manifest, their true nature is known only to you and to God. They are your secret until released through your actions.

It is also necessary for you to guard against self-deception. It is helpful to view objectively your actions and to test them carefully as to their true motivations. Perhaps as good a test as any is to examine the nature of your spiritual endeavors. That is, how many of them are carried on through doing those things which are silent and known only to you and to God, such as regular prayer work and meditation, and otherwise doing your works in such a way as to keep them completely anonymous, if at all possible.

Should you find that you are doing things in such a way as to make certain they are noticed by others, or that are certain to draw attention and recognition to yourself, or for reward or praise in any form, it would be exceedingly wise for you to make a careful and honest appraisal of your motives. Indeed, should these be your actions, it is suggested that you immediately alter your actions as to avoid the temptation to yield to the motives which have led you into such conduct.

No doubt you see the importance of the need to test your motives. Indeed, this is your responsibility. And when you discover selfishness motivating any of your purposes, the duty arises immediately for you to expunge this from your conscious efforts. An excellent technique for this is to concentrate upon only those ways which shall allow you to give selflessly of your love to others. As you do this, you also build up your defenses against the influences that would divert you from seeking only after such purposes.

An essential step towards being capable of service is the adequate preparation therefor. Thus it is necessary to clear away those obstacles which may hinder the flow of God's love through you. Indeed, this is your paramount function when you serve. You provide the means, the instrumentality, through which God manifests His Presence, His Love and Power to all you are able to reach. The more open you are, the better. Obviously, your motives are an integral quality of how well you meet this capability.

Each single effort made towards this purpose, is an important influence for good in your life and in the lives of all the others involved with you. Even those efforts which may seem small and insignificant at the moment, do a good work. For it is the willingness, the trying, the overt commitment to this purpose which carries with it the power of its source — the power of God's love.

It is this same power which gives the lasting and beneficent strength to the prayers you give for the healing and well-being of others, to the acts of kindness, large or small, you quietly and humbly give to those in need. Every act of kindness, friendliness, usefulness and assistance, when motivated by the selflessness to which we speak, is a magnificent service to your fellow man and to the Father. Do not dwell in the mistaken belief that one only serves God through large and magnanimous acts of generosity, for this is not the case at all. Certainly, such actions are often praiseworthy, but, more frequently than not, they are motivated and prompted by selfishness.

The ultimate test, dearly beloved brethren, is what comes from the heart. Those actions which are brought about by your will and desire to serve God and your fellow man in love and in thanksgiving to God that He may be glorified, are truly blessed and sanctified. And you are indeed blessed, dear brethren, when you bring yourself to consciously pursue such purposes.

Even now, as you read these words, you experience an increased quickening of the Light within your heart center, and the radiance and vibrations it gives forth are noticeably greater. There comes to your heart an awareness of an even deeper acceptance of the dedication you have made to be more Christlike in every aspect of your life. We pray to the Father that His Power within you shall continue to unfold and to manifest more clearly unto all mankind.

As you undertake each day of your Earth life to try as best you can to hold to these principles and make them a part of your life, each single effort in that direction brings a great flow of the Father's love into your life. Thus the blessing of His love is already a reality in the fruits of your endeavors. Thus, you need not wait until you have reached the perfection for which you strive in order to receive of the Father's blessed love; it is already with you!

Is it any wonder, then, that we should constantly and continuously proclaim the beauty of the Father's love? Indeed, the answer should be clear for you. Take of His love, beloved brethren, but also give freely and abundantly of it unto all in your midst; for this, too, is a function of that love.

Chapter 8

THE LAW OF FORGIVENESS

*For when you have thus forgiven your brother you
have given forgiveness for the Father; for you have
given love and that which is love is of the Father.*

WE WOULD speak upon an aspect of love—the important Law of Forgiveness.

In the prayer taught by the Master Jesus, this
principle is set forth in a brief and concisely stated form.
But do not let the brevity of its form mislead you or
detract from its importance. For this teaching, like all
the teachings of the Beloved Master, is filled with great
Truth.

"Forgive us our debts (trespasses) as we forgive our
debtors (trespassers)." Notice there is no language included in this statement which takes from your obligation and responsibility to forgive others.

The doctrines and teachings of many religions assert a
broad and liberal assurance of the Father's forgiveness of
the sins of men; especially in connection with the doctrine of vicarious atonement. And indeed this great beneficent act of love flowing from the Father is a fact and He
does give forgiveness.

But it is imperative that all men understand that this
principle of forgiveness, this cleansing flow of love, must
first originate with the individual. Notice, the Master
does not say, "Forgive us our debts *and* our debtors" but
"*As we forgive* our debtors." "For if ye forgive men their
trespasses, your heavenly Father will also forgive you: But

if ye forgive not men their trespasses, neither will your Father forgive your trespasses."

Thus, the Master clearly sets forth the law. He who seeks forgiveness must first give forgiveness to his brother. *As* he first forgives, is he to be forgiven.

Perhaps you have observed that this principle is doing much to carry out another law and principle with which you are familiar — the law of Cause and Effect. For by the power of the act of forgiveness, which you have first set into motion, you bring unto yourself an effect formed of this power; thus of like effect. Your initial act served to set into motion the processes governed by this principle and law.

True enough, the Father always stands ready to give of His forgiveness, for this is the very nature of His love. But it remains necessary for you to provide the first step that triggers this principle into action. And this you do by and through *your* act of forgiveness.

The Master gives this teaching several times over and we would direct your attention to them, suggesting that you meditate upon them. And, as you do this, you shall find an ever deeper insight into the significance of this law and principle. Forgive, and expect forgiveness as you have forgiven. And not until you have forgiven, should you expect to be forgiven.

In your external world, this principle is not observed or followed by many people. Indeed, most worldly relationships are still governed by the old law of "an eye for an eye, and a tooth for a tooth." Everyone seeks redress for whatever wrongs they may claim to have suffered. And while this practice conforms to man's law, it does not give obedience to God's law of forgiveness. Indeed, this is not forgiveness and does nothing to teach forgiveness. Rather, it breeds and fosters the opposite attitudes and feelings of resentment, hate, anger and fear.

You, beloved brethren, have come a long way along the paths you have chosen. However, it is suggested that you make it a point from time to time, and especially while within the silence of your inner self, to examine carefully the nature of your secret thoughts and feelings. Do you find within them any thoughts or feelings of vindictiveness or resentment towards another? Are there any feelings of hurt, sadness, or sorrow, perhaps, growing out of events in and from which you feel you have been wronged, and thus justified in harboring anger and resentment against those responsible? Or do you feel that you have been mistreated in a manner not at all deserved, and thus entitled to be angry?

Think back over your life, recall to your mind occasions when you felt others had harmed you in some way. Have you since forgiven them? You may have said to them directly, or silently within your heart and mind, "I forgive you," but have you truly forgiven them? Or do you continue to carry a hurt feeling about what they did to you? Are you harboring some resentment over this?

If there are any such remnants of those events remaining, whatever they may be, there has been no real forgiveness. To forgive means to conclude completely the event, to release completely, from all thought and memory, everything that happened, including all feelings of harm or injury, whether thought as justified or not.

If these, or similar thoughts and feelings, are present in your consciousness to any degree, or in any form, then you should know that you have not given obedience to the Law of Forgiveness.

When you say to another, "I forgive you," show forgiveness through love, through prayer, through actions founded in love. When you so give of your love, resentment cannot remain alive, nor can feelings of hurt and self-pity remain within your heart. There is a vast difference between *speaking* forgiveness and *giving* forgiveness.

It is essential, however, that you also give time and thought to the principles of Causation and Compensation and thus remember that all things have their purpose; that each act, each occurrence, each event is a link, one with the other, in the chain of your life. And rather than continue to hold onto old hurts, sorrows, and resentments, and the negative effects they hold over you, release them, turn them loose by the beautiful cleansing power of forgiveness.

This is so much easier said than done, this we know. But, sooner or later, my beloved, you must learn to give complete obedience to this law, when it shall become a continuing and constant practice of your life. And the more quickly you make this endeavor, the better it shall be for all concerned.

Perhaps you may think that what we have said here is nothing new. Nevertheless, what we say is profoundly important to what you do with your life. The Initiates, the Blessed Ones, long ago learned of the need to practice total and complete forgiveness.

Persevere in your efforts. Practice the disciplines that come through the dynamics of this principle. Each time you truly, freely, voluntarily, and without any thought at all of reward or recompense, give forgiveness to the debt or trespass of another, you immediately sense the cleanliness and the beauty of the White Light of the Father's Love as it courses throughout all your being in a fervent and deeply-felt blessing from Him.

And there is yet another whom you must forgive; that one is yourself. Do not let feelings of guilt over past misdeeds and mistakes cause you harm and hold you back in your growth, for you must learn also to give release unto yourself from those happenings, especially those for which you have made amends and have been forgiven. This is not to say that you are to gloss over misbehavior, but it is a mistake to hang onto the past and its mistakes and misdeeds because this can lead to a self-imposed false sense of martyrdom, which can be indeed harmful.

As you view this moment which gives you so strongly the sense of a truly new beginning of a new phase in your life, why not resolve to begin it upon a firm foundation, upon the principle of Brotherhood? You could choose no better way to move than to seek with all earnestness and desire to make application of this principle to your life.

And so, we would suggest, beloved brethren, that you be resolved that no thought shall be entertained, or word spoken, or act committed unless it is such as would meet this test. Remember always to do unto others as you would have them do unto you. If your contemplated thoughts and actions are of this nature, then, freely send them forth.

As you must see, this truth is founded upon love, as is all truth. This principle teaches quite simply the giving of kindness and love. Indeed, as you seek after truth you shall always find that all relationships which bring peace, contentment and joy to their participants have their existence founded in and are supported by this principle. Whenever man brings the power of this truth to the level where it is the motivation of his life, he finds that beautiful and lasting relationships are always the fruits of his endeavors.

Therefore, let yourself rise above the worldly and material things of your life. Always keep your eyes upon the Christ Star. Aspire to become ever purer in your daily living that the Christ Light within may become your guiding star in all your affairs.

Make this a day of joy, of praise and thanksgiving. Indeed, we give thanks unto the Father-Mother God that we may meet with you and enfold you in our love. This, to us, is a blessing from the Father, that we may know you, and the many others to whom we can go, and share in God's many and abundant blessings.

Chapter 9

STUDY AS A MEANS
TO HIGHER SPIRITUAL ATTAINMENT

*I am the door: by me if any man enter in, he shall
be saved, and shall go in and out, and find pasture.*
(John 10:9)

WE HAVE chosen these words of the Christ Jesus for
the theme of this chapter because of the value
they possess in bringing before you the suggestion
we have earlier made of your need to examine carefully
into the teachings of the Master Jesus that you may gain
the deeper meanings in them.

While it is not our purpose to teach you to read into
His words, or ours, meanings which are not there, nor
reasonably deducible from them, we do renew our suggestion that it would be wise for you to seek out the esoteric meanings that are included in them. Through this
practice, you add to your understanding and wisdom,
also you increase your ability to discern and to seek out
the truths which shall add to your opportunities for spiritual unfoldment.

Jesus gave many of His teachings through parables,
and we are bewildered over the fact that throughout the
hundreds of years which have followed His ministry on
Earth, so few have made any real effort to understand
and to teach their meanings. We especially have in mind
the failure of the churches to do this. It is amazing to

observe how little attention is given to the esoteric, the inner meanings and principles which Jesus seeks to show man about life.

For example, let us examine the parable from which our theme has been taken. A literal meaning of the parable may be as follows: Jesus says He is the "shepherd" and man is the "sheep," and, through following after Him, man may properly enter through the "door" into the "sheepfold" and thus be saved. While such a succinct interpretation carries with it a message of spiritual importance, we would suggest that the parable is teaching considerably more than this. We make another interpretation we believe is deducible from what is said.

Jesus likely has in mind that "sheep," as used here, does not represent "man" at all. But, instead, is denoting a part of man, the emotional aspects of man's being, that which proceeds from the lower self and manifests as the human and animalistic nature of his being. The "sheepfold" represents the "kingdom of heaven" within man, wherein he finds God, wherein he taps into the Universal Intelligence, the Cosmic Father-Mother. The term "door" represents the Christ Spirit both as manifested through Jesus, and as rests within the heart center of all men.

If we use these meanings, we begin to see a deeper teaching unfolding to us. We find that Jesus again proclaims, but in slightly different form, that as man submits to the urgings of the Christ Light within—the Higher Self of his being—and undertakes to follow the guidance he receives from this Source, he shall overcome and bring under control the influence and power which constantly flows from his lower nature, his lower self. Thus he becomes released and "saved" from the ensnaring grasp and hold the lower, materially and worldly oriented part of his being has upon his life. He is "saved" from the throes of darkness which hold him captive within the bonds of earthly illusion and desire.

The "life" that the "good shepherd" gives for his sheep is the surrender you make to "the quickening within" that compels you to give up the "old self" which has for so long been only of the material and physical world. And until this part of you dies the Christ within is not free to ascend and rule and bring forth Its Light.

Moreover, this phenomenon of growth—the death of the worldly and material aspect and the ascension of the spiritual—ultimately comes to each individual and is the experience and accomplishment of the soul. For, as it is stated, "But he that is an hireling, and not the shepherd, whose own the sheep are not, seeth the wolf coming (the influence and force of evil both from within and from without) and leaveth the sheep, and fleeth: and the wolf catcheth them, and scattereth the sheep."

Indeed, dearly beloved, let it be made clear to your understanding that the responsibility for growing into ever purer and higher levels and planes of Light and consciousness belongs to each one individually. While it should be the desire and purpose of all to be of service and help to one another, no one may do for the other those things which are fixed as the responsibility of each. Each phase of soul-growth is an individual responsibility.

This brings us to discuss briefly the relationship existing between you and us. We, your brothers, who serve as your guides, your Guardian Angels, having assumed this responsibility in your behalf, are always with you. We always strive to give you our love, and to do whatever we can to direct you more nearly along the paths which are best for you. We are, however, necessarily limited in how far we may go and in what we may do for you. For we are subject to the same principles governing the Father's Creation as are you.

We, of course, see your mistakes. And, when this happens, we wish deeply that you would open yourself to the guidance we are sending you that you would do differently. But this is as far as we can go. To go beyond this by compelling you to do as we direct, we would be doing for you that which you must learn to do for yourself. We never seek to force anything upon you. No one of spirit, save perhaps those who come from darkness, ever seek to force their will upon anyone.

I am not permitted to force anything upon Philip. Indeed, these words he speaks and writes, I give through him. But if he were to close his mind to me and my thoughts, or refuse to receive what I seek to channel through him, I would not force him to receive them. No more so than would any of your guides attempt to force their thoughts upon you. True enough, we may repeat many times certain suggestions, first in one form and then in another, hoping that they shall be received and followed. But the choice to receive them and to follow them remains always with you.

The thoughts of goodness which come to your mind, as well as those of an evil nature, come both from within and from without your own being. Each of you, presently being possessed of duality of being, is capable of both good and evil; this you have experienced and should know. Your Higher Self and lower self are sources of thoughts. Similarly, you may receive the thoughts and impressions we seek to give you, as do the dark ones about you. But the choice is yours as to which you will receive and make as your own. And this is a responsibility you cannot assign to anyone else, the decisions you make need to be your own. This is one reason why teachings are given to you many times over, especially those which caution you of the many pitfalls flowing from the illusions of the physical and material world about you.

We are hopeful that you shall follow the guidance which comes from your Higher Self, and from that which we are permitted to place before you. We know, however, that should you refuse to follow this form of guidance, or elect to follow some other way, sooner or later, you will find yourself back at this same point on your path, and, remembering the experiences you have gained, choose to follow the proper way. This is one very effective way to learn discernment. You can be shown and told what to do, but ordinarily this alone is not sufficient to give you the experiences your soul seeks to have and to gain. Only the life you live can give you the personal experiences and knowledge then needed. The decisions you are called upon to make, the sense of judgment you learn to exercise in the various situations thus presented, operate to give you the opportunities necessary to bring you the wisdom you seek.

Perhaps this is a good time to point out one further aspect with reference to the guidance your invisible brothers are giving to you. Do not labor under the belief that such guidance always comes to you in a direct and straightforward manner. Frequently it is given in subtle and hidden form. This may come as a surprise to some, however, the wisdom of this practice becomes evident as you move forward in your spiritual quest.

You may have at some time wondered over what the underlying purposes may be for your having taken this incarnation. If you should do this, you may begin to have a greater appreciation of this arrangement which exists between you and your guides. Through the form of life incarnate you are provided a specific means of gaining spiritual wisdom and growth which is not attainable in any other way. But this growth does not ordinarily come about unless you affirmatively strive for it. Learning to actively use the power of your mind—a powerful tool entrusted to you by the Father—is an important step. Indeed, failing or refusing to do this is worse than misusing it.

Far too many expect their "guides" to provide the answers to all the problems they may face, or to direct their every step. And, unfortunately, there are entities in spirit who endeavor to oblige, or they lead the incarnate to think they are receiving correct guidance when they are not. It should be evident to you that such a "guide" would be doing harm rather than good.

If your brothers in spirit make all your decisions and solve all your problems, what do you gain from such experiences? While a measure of growth comes to your spiritual brethren from the special experience they gain in serving as a guide, this does not give them any right or occasion to "live the life" of their incarnate brethren for them. Indeed, they gain far more wisdom through the anxieties and sufferings they endure while observing their incarnate brethren's failure to receive and follow the guidance they have set before them.

We would suggest, dear brethren, that you avoid the temptation to rely *exclusively* upon the advice, counsel, or decisions appearing to come from a spirit guide or entity. You never learn discernment by accepting at face value all that comes from spirit. Discernment is learned by examining, testing and weighing carefully all that is received, and by listening to the "still small voice within." You must learn to use your own mind and exercise common sense. Indeed, you must learn to utilize *all* your talents, lest they atrophy and become lost to you.

It may seem that we digress from our theme, however, we would demonstrate that there are valid reasons underlying the practice of hiding spiritual truth, guidance, and the mysteries of life in parables and subtle form. This practice has long been generously employed among those segments of the populace who were genuinely bent upon finding the truth and utilizing the powers gained from this for the benefit of mankind generally, and not for personal gain or misdirected use. Were there no cause for this, the Master Jesus, and all teachers before Him, and since, would not have used these forms of dispensing such knowledge. We also employ this method of teaching. Rather than to delve more deeply into the purposes for this practice, we here quote from the teachings of Jesus, as recorded in your Holy Bible, that you may determine for yourself the significance His words bear to what we say.

> *"And the disciples came, and said unto him, Why speakest thou unto them in parables?*
> *"He answered and said unto them, Because it is given unto you to know the mysteries of the kingdom of heaven, but to them it is not given.*
> *"For whosoever hath, to him shall be given, and he shall have more abundance: but whosoever hath not, from him shall be taken away even that he hath.*
> *"Therefore speak I to them in parables: because they seeing see not; and hearing they hear not, neither do they understand.*
> *"And in them is fulfilled the prophecy of Esaias, which saith, By hearing ye shall hear, and shall not understand; and seeing ye shall see, and shall not perceive:*
> *"For this people's heart is waxed gross, and their ears are dull of hearing, and their eyes they have closed; lest at any time they should see with their eyes, and hear with their ears, and should understand with their heart, and should be converted, and I should heal them.*
> *"But blessed are your eyes, for they see: and your ears, for they hear.*
> *"For verily I say unto you, That many prophets and righteous men have desired to see those things which ye see, and have not seen them; and to hear those things which ye hear, and have not heard them."*

Also:

> *"Give not that which is holy unto the dogs, neither cast ye your pearls before swine, lest they trample them under their feet, and turn again and rend you.*

"Ask, and it shall be given you; seek, and ye shall find; knock, and it shall be opened unto you:

"For every one that asketh receiveth; and he that seeketh findeth; and to him that knocketh it shall be opened."

Now we take up again our interpretation of the parable and teaching of Jesus we have chosen as the subject of this chapter.

What meaning should be ascribed to the words: "and shall go in and out, and find pasture?" Since this is defining that which "man" should do, it would be strange to say that "man" would need "pasture," for this obviously more properly describes the husbandry interests man would have for his animals; in this instance, his sheep. But since the term "pasture" does pertain to a source of food for animals, it is reasonable to attribute to the term, in the context used, the meaning of: "Spiritual food."

Thinking back to the earlier literal interpretation, it would seem logical to postulate the premise that once man was able to find his way through the "door" into the "sheepfold" of heaven, he most likely would not wish to leave and go back out.

It, therefore, seems to be more fitting to look at the phrase, "Shall go in and out" as describing a means of reaching "the kingdom of heaven within" through the practice of meditation, perhaps, by which man is given the means of reaching his Source of spiritual food: The Higher Self. By going through the "door" to the Higher Self—the Christ within—man truly finds the wisdom and the strength with which to shepherd the "sheep" of his own being. Thus can he be made whole in the Light of the Love of God, the Father-Mother. Truly, he finds pasture for his whole being.

But we ask that you make your own analysis and study of this parable. Take our thoughts into your meditations, however, you should not close off any other interpretation that you receive. Indeed, we would suggest that you frequently use the parables of the Master Jesus as the subject of your meditations, looking forward to the new insights which are likely to come to you from this practice.

After a time, go back to this parable and study it carefully again and meditate upon it. You shall find that new and added meanings and significances shall come from this practice. As you grow spiritually, your sense of values changes. And a new insight into the deeper "things of life" brings about new interests and enthusiasm for gaining greater understanding in all things.

Indeed, we call your attention to what Jesus said concerning the many prophets and righteous men who had not seen or heard those things seen and heard by the Apostles. Notice His use of the word "desired"—they had "desired" to see and to hear but had not seen or heard. We suggest that this makes it very clear that to only "desire" these attributes is not enough, there needs to be more.

The Master promises that if one asks, he shall receive; if he seeks, he shall find; and if he knocks, it shall be opened unto him. Observe that each of these steps requires affirmative action, and each is a different form of action. Also observe that they are set forth in a conjunctive manner, not disjunctively. Thus, it is necessary that *all three* be undertaken that "it (the door?) shall be opened to you."

Dearly beloved brethren, we seek to incite you into greater activity designed to lead you to higher spiritual attainment. Obviously, determined study and consideration of what our Lord Christ teaches is an appropriate part of that activity. We are hopeful that what we have given you will stir you into greater action along these lines. We also hold the added hope that you will make the principles of Love and Brotherhood as demonstrated and taught by Jesus the active purpose of your daily living.

Chapter 10

BALANCE AND HARMONY

Look to nature, for there you may find yourself.
Look within yourself, and there you shall find God.

T HE nature of your thoughts and your attitudes frequently appears to us as the surface of a great sea.
When they are calm and of even disposition, your
vibrations and energy fields are as a calm sea. There is a
gentle swell — a gentle rising and lowering of the energy
flow, a smooth and regular pulsation of the energy flowing in a smooth cyclic wave form. And these waves flow
on and on, ultimately reaching the shore with a gentle
caress and release of the energy they have carried. So
do your thoughts, which emanate from a calm and
peaceful mind, gently carry their energy to their intended destination.

Then, when there is upset, or when the emotions are
restless and disturbed, they appear much as the sea when
it is disturbed by turbulent weather and forces, which, if
allowed to continue, shall cause the surface to build into
towering and destructive waves that crash forcefully
against everything in their path, leaving harm and injury
in their wake. So, also do the thoughts and attitudes
flowing from minds that are caught up in conditions of
disturbing unrest, emotional upset and anger, leave
harm and injury in their wake.

It is obvious that a great difference in the form of the energy is observed, and should be expected to flow from such differing states of attitude and thought.

Included in this comparison between an aspect of nature and the human mind, is the suggestion that you may, from this demonstration, gain added insight into why the Master Jesus so frequently used the sea, and other objects of nature, for His teachings, both as a symbol and as a part of his environment.

Indeed, if you look about you to the beautiful creation into which you have been placed, you see demonstrated in many forms the same forces and influences flowing into and from them as occur in and affect your own life. And, just as you may observe in nature the stilling and quieting influences which prevail because of the harmonious and balancing qualities divinely ordained in the natural phenomenon of the Father's creation, so, too, do you find within yourself similar powers and forces acting upon you and through you; their ultimate effects being determined by the quality of harmony and balance you contribute by your own disciplines and power of self-control.

Perhaps you have already realized that of the principal lessons to be learned in your incarnations on the Earth plane, self-control, self-discipline, and harmonious relationships with your fellow man, your environment, and yourself, are among the most important.

Thus you find frequent reminders coming both from us and from other sources which point out that it is wise for you to expect to find many challenges and difficult situations to contend with during your Earth life. For to grow in your ability to acquire and maintain this quality of self-control and harmony, you must be willing to work out karmic debts and to accept the added responsibilities this requires.

While it may seem reasonable to expect that such experiences would necessarily foreclose or impede your finding much happiness and peace while upon the Earth plane, we would say that this need not be the case at all. Indeed, it is intended that you are to learn to find and enjoy much happiness and peace in this incarnation, but that it is earned by what you do.

The extent to which peace and happiness may be a part of your life is determined primarily by the extent to which you are able to put into active practice in your daily living the principles of Love and Brotherhood and Service. Unless these are brought into your life through your own conscious effort, harmony — and its by-products of peace and happiness — may be somewhat difficult for you to come by.

But as you endeavor to carry these efforts forward, you shall find a growing sense of peace and quiet entering into your life. To the point that one day you shall find that you have developed the keen ability to remain calm, tranquil and peaceful, even while being lashed by the fury of the stormy sea of disturbed human emotion all about you. For you will have introduced these principles of divine truth as the principal motivation of your life and to have begun reaping the harvest of good they can bring you.

Truth is light. Light is love. And love has within it the peace, harmony, quiet and stillness which prevails always over all else which would destroy it. The truism expressed by the Old Testament Psalmist: "Be still and know that *I am* God," provides a key to this all-important principle.

There are times when you are in better and closer attunement with us; and we are able to reach you more easily as well. While other circumstances and conditions may have their effect, the quality of such attunement is determined in great measure by your attitudes and by the extent to which your love is flowing from you.

When we speak of love in this sense, we intend specifically to stress the energy aspect involved. For, in this respect, love is a profound energy, a form of energy of the greatest good imaginable. It has been described as being the cohesive force of the universe. It is that energy which is used to bring about attunement, a coming together, a closeness, a reaching of one heart to another.

It is this part of life which is so important and so necessary towards the evolvement and unfoldment of the spiritual nature of mankind. This is what the Beloved Master Jesus teaches and gives to His disciples and followers. Indeed, we seek to carry on this same principle with you.

The Brotherhood of man. Oh, how often has this been preached! This has so often been expressed, but has fallen upon ears that would not hear, placed before eyes which would not see, and presented to minds that were closed or refused to receive it. Yet, in spite of man's failures, little by little, and slowly but surely, he is coming to learn and to understand what this really means to him.

We speak on this theme, dear ones, for several reasons. The principal one being that we would have you be ever mindful of the love you are, the love you have, and the love you must give to your fellow man. The love you have within you is not for you to keep, or to hold on to, or to hoard as you would a treasure. It is to be given away, to be given unto others; *then,* it truly becomes a treasure for you!

Thus, we come back once again to what has been earlier expressed concerning the importance of meditation. Indeed, this practice provides an excellent form of endeavor which fosters and develops self-discipline. For, as you learn to control your thoughts and emotions, there is awakened within you certain powers and strengths which will do much, and rather quickly too, towards changing the situations, events and attitudes which have previously produced disharmony into more harmonious events and acitivities which are enjoyable and productive.

We realize that these things are not easy to do, and that they do not come about overnight. But we do know and promise you this: As you persevere in such endeavor, self-discipline improves with each attempt and each experience. You also gain in a willingness and the ability to be more patient with yourself, as well as with others. Indeed, patience is a companion of peace. Where you find one, you always find the other.

All these virtues, the beauties of God's creation, which you can turn to for help, guidance and example, and all the beautiful aspects of living you seek to bring into manifestation in your life, shall ultimately come together into one magnificently beautiful state of being. Thus, the power and blessing of love becomes the full expression of your life.

Oh, such a great order! Yet, it shall be fulfilled. As you strive towards that fulfillment, you observe that the Father does not wait for you to attain that goal before you may have His gift of love. Even though you may still be a far way off, He has, nevertheless, come out to meet you and given you abundantly of His love.

The thoughts coursing through your mind are much as a stream of water. If they are bright, clean and vibrant with love, they sparkle as a beautiful fresh mountain stream sending forth a joyful sound, as it bubbles over the polished stones beneath its surface, joining with the lilting songs of the birds and the beauty of the Father's creation all about it.

The thoughts which are positive and for good are strong and forceful and flow quickly. And, much as a heavy current, their strength carries the burdens placed upon them easily and quickly to their destination. While those that are not of this quality, but which are of a negative or evil nature, are much as a polluted stream which has become sluggish, filled with all forms of trash, debris and garbage, yielding little, if any, useful purpose, except to those who would pollute it even more.

And the mind that allows itself to be caught up into only selfish motive and purpose becomes in time as the stream which has had its flow halted by a dam, or other obstruction placed across it. As the flow is halted, it becomes stagnant and as a "Dead Sea."

This beautiful gift of the Father — your mind, a profound instrument of power — needs to be left open and free to receive and to express all of the thoughts, ideas and understanding intended for you both to receive and to send forth.

So be aware of this need and be quick to remove any blockage or obstruction to the ready flow of the energy of thought and idea.

Similarly, it is your responsibility — and it is a great one — to always exercise vigilance over the thoughts you may entertain or express, that they may remain free from the "pollution" which could cause harm to others, or to yourself.

For, as you have observed from your own experiences, to rid your rivers and streams of the pollution they have received is sometimes a very difficult undertaking; much more so than had effective and corrective measures first been followed. And so it is with your mind. Early attention to the control of the nature and quality of the thoughts flowing through and from it, though at times difficult to bring about because of the self-discipline involved, is, nevertheless, the much easier solution than to let it first become out of control and polluted.

In any event, the responsibility to maintain the purity of the "waters of the spirit" which flow through your mind, is yours. And the choice to meet that responsibility is also yours to make.

MEDITATION:
ON BALANCE AND HARMONY

Now, beloved brethren, relax and come with me into meditation. Visualize before you a beautiful wood of tall majestic pine and spruce dotted with colorful aspen and other flora. As you enter into the wood it is as though you have entered through the portals of a magnificent and hallowed cathedral. The sound of the wind in the trees, mingled with the songs of the birds, and the rustling of the leaves, is harmonious and peacefully uplifting. Breathe in the clean crisp mountain air perfumed with the fragrance of the trees and the many blossoms which border upon the placid waters of a small circular lake centered within our cathedral forest. The fragrances rise as incense to the Heavenly Throne above. Floating upon the surface of the crystal clear water of the lake are many other beautiful blossoms, among them the white lotus blossom, the sacred flower of India.

As you take in the wondrous beauty all about you, think of the Creator of all this, and give thanks for the many gifts you have received. Indeed, beloved ones, know that you may find your own flower in the Garden of Peace on a higher plane.

Now, as you look to the beautiful little lake, you see that the brilliant blue of the sky is reflected from it rendering it into the most beautiful blue you have ever seen. Suddenly there appear a host of angels, bringing with them many who are to be healed. The angels gently take their patients through the blue waters and they are healed. The thought comes to you that you, too, can bathe in these waters and be healed.

As you meditate upon this thought there appears above all of you the form of the Master Jesus. He can be seen at the moment of healing in His Body of Light. And thus you come to know and to understand that as you have attuned yourself to the Higher Realms you, too, may see the Christ in His Body of Light.

We suggest that you pause now and meditate upon this which we have given to you.

⊕

We bring you teachings, beloved brethren, that have been handed down throughout the ages—in every mystery school of the East. Man is a three-fold being, body, soul and spirit. Man is a creation of God, he is also the universe in Nature. And as you proceed with your spiritual development, you will realize that there is a point of contact within yourselves with the planetary system, with all creation. Each one has within himself the intelligence to understand his affinity with all creation and with the universal Life. Man has within himself also the power to be harmonious and peaceful towards all others and towards all circumstances around him.

Harmony is the soul of God, beloved ones. Therefore learn to be harmonious. Learn to be peaceful within yourselves, and keep absolute harmony on the Earth-plane. Play a simple melody of the soul, and when faced with conditions of life over which you have no control, or when people around you become inharmonious, do not let a discordant note sound through yourselves. Attune yourselves to the note of Christ, and all disharmony shall immediately fade away. This is so, beloved brethren, and it is for you to do and see that our words are true.

Perfection and wholeness are God's desire for all His creatures, for all humanity. Singleness of purpose and a consecrated life will enable each one to be a pure channel of God's service. Is it not better to voice the highest and carry forth the Light? Therefore, beloved ones, live in harmony within your Spirit, and live the life of Christ, the life that He lived upon the Earth-plane. You will go forth, then, carrying peace and goodwill to all mankind. This is God's perfect plan for the redemption of the world. Out of darkness comes light. The seed dies that it may live again. It remains hidden that it may function from within. Out of the weakness, strength. Remember this. Remember these things, dear brethren of Earth, in your journey on the path—the upward path of spiritual enlightenment.

Therefore, go calmly and peacefully upon your way, keeping harmony always in your daily life and peace within your heart. Perhaps, the relative, neighbor and friend, and others amongst whom you pass, will realize that you have something they have not, and will wonder what it is. But then they will realize that you are carrying a Light, a Light that will shed Its blessing upon all within Its radiance.

And so we leave you, dear ones. We leave you with love; we leave you in God's keeping. And in stillness let us raise ourselves to the Great Light, and to Love and Wisdom. We think of love, and we give, according to our understanding, the Light and the Love within our hearts.

And now, we sign you with the Sign of the Cross, and we enclose you in the Circle of the Great White Brotherhood, and we leave you in God's keeping, beloved. May peace be upon each one. Peace. Peace. Peace. Amen.

Chapter 11

POWER OF THOUGHT

Brethren, whatsoever things are true, whatsoever things are honest, whatsoever things are just, whatsoever things are pure, whatsoever things are lovely, whatsoever things are of good report; if there be any virtue, and if there be any praise, think on these things. Philippians 4:8

ALREADY much has been written and spoken upon the subject of "thought;" indeed, we, too, have given much attention to this subject. Nevertheless, its importance merits further attention from us.

An accompanying matter of equal importance which must be considered with the subject of "thought" is the ever present, supremely important all-encompassing law of Cause and Effect. It has equal application to the nature of thought as it does to everything else you send forth.

If what we say seems repetitious to you, we would suggest that before you lay this aside or pay any less attention to what is said, you first assay your own thoughts and honestly evaluate them as to their purity. Are they selfless and charitable to others? Are they within the perimeters of conduct suggested by the commandments of the Beloved Master Jesus as concerns your relationships with your fellow man? Are they without need of improvement in any respect? Will you welcome them back gladly as they return to you in like or similar form? If a self-examination of this nature permits you to make affirmative aswers to these or similar questions, then, obviously, you have progressed very far spiritually and would perhaps be above anything we might here place before you.

On the other hand, we would venture to say that you likely shall welcome the opportunity to review these matters. Perhaps, a deeper understanding, if not new understandings and insight may come from this. For, as we have said earlier, we seek to set before you those things which give you truth, and we find that much of it needs to be repeated. Thus you may come to understand more clearly their meanings and take them into your heart.

Man has received from God no greater privilege than the right and the power of thought. Indeed, with this gift, God has given man the power of creation—the power to use his will to bring forth whatsoever he chooses, be it good or evil. For, by his thoughts, he controls the direction his will shall take.

If you consider this one aspect alone, you must conclude that through this gift, if for no other reason—and there are many—God has demonstrated His great love for you.

For centuries, man has debated the source of his thoughts, seeking to determine if they have their source in the mind, the soul, or from some other place such as a universal intelligence, mind, or soul. But regardless of their source originally, it should be understood that you, the individual who issues forth the thought, are responsible for the form it takes at its emanation and its being loosed as an expressed thought. To be otherwise would allow you to escape responsibility for what you alone have sent forth in your thoughts. No one other than yourself has control over what the thought is to be, therefore, you must be ready to assume the responsibilities that go with the privilege of the use of the power of thought.

Thoughts are things, living things, frequently described as a form of energy. Yet it is amazing to behold how very many believe that their thoughts are as nothing, especially those thoughts which do not culminate in some manifested word or act. This misconception leads many into difficulty.

While thoughts not yet manifested into some physical expression are invisible to the physical eye, they, nevertheless, may be very real. If persisted in, they will sooner or later crystallize into a visible form fitting the essence of their creation. Perhaps the crystallization will occur with the one to whom the thoughts were directed, whereas, in every instance, this crystallization process can be expected to occur with the one originating the thoughts. And, in the latter instance, the crystallization always takes the form represented by the nature of the thoughts.

Ask yourself, "What have I created today?" We suggest this as a means of impressing upon you the importance of your need to be extremely careful with how you use your power of thought. For truly this is a creative power that you use.

Pause for a moment and think about this: Everything you undertake to do first comes as a thought. There is no escaping this truth. The words you say, the actions you carry out, all have their beginning in this phenomenon of thought.

Look about your physical world. The buildings you see were first a thought of the architect or builder that was incorporated into plans and designs. The materials used in their construction were also first in the form of thoughts which grew into ideas, plans and designs that guided them into the physical form contemplated. The automobiles you operate are products of design, plan and idea. The roadways and streets upon which you drive, the walkways upon which you may walk, were all laid out and the composition of the component materials used in their construction came from plans and ideas which had their beginning in thought.

We could continue listing the numerous items with which you are in contact each day and, in each instance, you would find that each one was first a thought. Every object was first conceived as a thought in the mind of someone. Its creation did not "just happen." That which took physical form was first created in thought, conceived in the invisible processes of the mind and intelligence of the creator.

Now let us approach this in another way, in the form of another question. If everything having being was first a thought, then is it correct to assume that every thought will become a creation appropriate to its concept? Or, to put it a little differently, does every thought always create that which it has embodied as a thought? As we answer "yes" to each of these questions, we wish to make clear the understanding that the point we are discussing here is primarily in relation to the effect of man's thoughts upon himself. We have in mind especially those situations where certain thoughts have persisted over a considerable period of time, rather than a situation dealing only with fleeting or isolated thoughts, but even these can reach a level of substantial impact under certain conditions.

As you make this closer examination into this aspect of your being, it is important that you realize the full part your thoughts play in your life; indeed, that they are involved in controlling your circumstances, your health, your character, your spiritual endeavors. Every other aspect of your life is the product of your own creation, the product of your own thoughts.

No man is at his present place in life by chance or accident. All facets of your existence are governed by universal, divine law. That which surrounds you in the way of circumstance and environment is that which you have caused to be there. Indeed, the character you manifest is but a reflection of what lies within your heart.

The thoughts which you may think are secretly harbored within your own heart shall, nevertheless, in due time crystallize into a manifested form. For the force and energy thus used ultimately renders its effect. This immutable law cannot be circumvented or avoided.

This brings us to point out that while the mind may be the principal instrumentality which processes the thought, the nature and purpose being expressed in the thought is determined by what comes from the heart. It can safely be said that each thought comes from within, whether it expresses that which is godly, or that which is evil. As Jesus says, "That which cometh out of man, that defileth the man. For from within, out of the heart of men, proceed evil thoughts . . . , Blessed are the pure in heart: for they shall see God."

We would make a few practical applications to what we have said.

Many of you have, at one time or another, considered entering into one of the "self-help" programs which employ processes of positive thinking. You were advised that by making thorough application of this technique, you were assured of a successful solution to your problems. We concur generally in that assurance as the theory and principles involved are genuine and really work. It is only that these programs generally are directed toward helping you "become a success in your business" or "the top salesman in your company." In a sense, this is unfortunate that this same effort is not directed into spiritual purposes, for the successes that could thus be attained there would enure also towards meeting your material needs.

Positive thinking and thoughts produce positive results, and negative thinking and negative thoughts produce negative results, either of which may readily be discerned from your countenance. An experiment you may wish to perform is with the use of a mirror. While looking into a mirror concentrate upon only happy and peaceful thoughts of good and joyful well-being. Watch the expressions reflected from your features, especially from your eyes. Now briefly concentrate only upon thoughts of sadness and sorrow and observe what happens to your features. Notice how they have changed.

Now go a step farther and think only of any prejudice or resentment you may hold, and of episodes of intense anger, and observe how quickly your countenance changes to reflect these forms of darkness. Look into your eyes, for they truly mirror what comes from within. Compare these reflections you have witnessed and discover that this simple test does indeed lend significance to what we have given you.

Godly thoughts and aspiration after true spiritual values crystallize into understanding and forbearance. They bring you a peace and calmness within which leads to greater insight and wisdom. There also comes about a deeper understanding of the realities of life and of your relationship with them and thus also with God.

Evil thoughts and thoughts only of worldly matters crystallize into deeper desires and feelings of selfishness and greed with a corresponding increase in lust after the immoral aspects of life. These may also lead to even greater entanglement in and enslavement to the illusionary life which is the product of a life committed only to material values.

It is therefore correct to say that, in great measure, man controls his own destiny by his thoughts. Indeed, every one who has undertaken, to some degree, to practice self-control and self-purification of his thoughts has noticed a decided change for the better occurring in the circumstances and events of his life. Never has it failed that as when one earnestly applies himself towards remedying his character defects and shortcomings, he makes "swift and marked progress, and passes rapidly through a succession of vicissitudes."

The aphorism of "like attracts like" has equal application here. For the nature and quality of your thoughts always attracts to you conditions and circumstances of like quality. As it has been written, "The soul attracts that which it secretly harbors; that which it loves, and also that which it fears; it reaches the height of its cherished aspirations; it falls to the level of its unchastened desires; and circumstances are the means by which the soul receives its own."

What is fear, but a condition of the mind built upon thoughts of apprehension, distrust, and lack of faith. And though they remain within the mind, and often secretly so, they, nevertheless, attract the very things they fear. Observe the regularity with which persons become afflicted with an illness or disease they have always feared greatly. The persistent presence of thoughts harboring such fear has served to attract rather than repel the malady.

The unfailing power of attraction works both ways. The harborer of thoughts and desires of charity and Christian love attracts to himself forces and individuals of like mind and purpose. Obviously, it would, therefore, be extremely wise to practice greater control over your form of thinking. For, as you do so, dear brethren, and learn to cast out those thoughts that are evil and harmful to yourself and to others, replacing them with positive and constructive ones, you shall experience an evergrowing sense of well-being and serenity, steeped in humble respect of your fellow man, and bathed in the light of God's love.

Through these efforts at purification of your thought processes, you, in fact, cleanse and purify that which wells up from within. Thus you transmute that which has been the source of evil into that which is good. Thus you remove the darkness from around your heart that the Divine Light of the Christ may radiate an ever increasing brilliance of the White Light, the Light of Love.

And so it is, dearly beloved, that you must recognize this power and strength which is yours. Perhaps it becomes clearer to your understanding of how it is your responsibility — indeed, your duty — to exercise this power of Self to rectify wrongs, to cleanse the mind, the heart and the soul of all impure thoughts, desires and purposes, seeking always to maintain a high degree of inner and mental aspiration after higher and greater spiritual attainment. It is admirable, indeed, to hold and harbor this ideal and vision. Having this as your goal, you shall move steadily forward in your spiritual growth. You shall improve not only your own spiritual stature, but you shall also affect beneficently all those around you who come within the influence of your Light. You cannot strive after spiritual virtue with an humble and grateful heart without also being of service both to God and to your fellow man.

Lest you be disappointed in your efforts, we would remind you that thought habits of long standing become fully entrenched and may require much greater attention and effort to be changed. So do not be disheartened by any recurrence of thought practices which earlier you may have considered as overcome. Rather, renew your efforts with even greater vigor through the knowledge that it is only by such effort that success is obtained; also, that much good comes from just your efforts alone. For each effort is witnessed by God, Who blesses them with His Love and Understanding.

Chapter 12

POWER OF PRAYER

Pray without ceasing.
(I Thessalonians 5:17)

A FTER understanding the power of thought, we find that its greatest impact is when you direct your thoughts to prayer. Prayer is one of the most creative thought processes you may practice.

We find that your prayers seem to take two main courses. When you are not involved in prayer over someone's health, you are involved in prayer over world peace. The following will explain the full potential of your prayers in both areas.

You have prayed for healing of your friends and loved ones and the many whose identity comes to you through only a name. The power of the prayers you have given has been that which flows from God's love. The light they have been given is abundant, fully endowed with the Father's grace. Your prayers have performed this function.

Frequently the question arises in the minds of men concerning the efficacy of prayer, and especially the prayers for healing, as you have given. It is the argument of some that they serve no good purpose; of others, that not all prayer is "answered" and of others, that they are all answered, but there are times when God says, "No."

As most of you know, it is not our purpose to cause or to create any conflict or disagreement; that we do not in

103

anyway seek to force our views upon anyone. For we believe that each one is entitled to his own opinions and view about such things according to his level of understanding. But we know that many are seeking greater understanding and deeper insight into matters of this nature, and therefore, we feel it appropriate to state our views on this question for whatever assistance it may give you in this area of interest.

We begin with the statement that all prayer is answered. But with that statement we add that there are a number of factors involved in this activity or function which contributes to or detracts from the effectiveness of it. So it is not wise to rely totally upon any single statement, such as this just given by us, without going further and examining, at least briefly, into what some of these other factors may be.

Obviously, the quality of the prayer itself does much to determine what its effectiveness may be. That is, how was it given? What prompted it? What motivations led to its being given? How selfless and free from thought of reward or recompense in any form were the thoughts underlying it? Was it voluntary or was it given in obedience to a sense or feeling of duty or obligation?

Every prayer given in love of one's fellow man and in complete selflessness transmits a great power. For it is indeed a gift from the one to the other of the Father's love. But this does not mean to say that any other prayer does not do good, or "reach its mark" as some would say.

If you would but pause for a moment and think upon this phenomenon, you shall realize that when one gives his effort and actions over to this act of praying, he is employing the power of his mind to express certain thoughts that are thus sent forth. Regardless of the promptings leading to this action, this individual has chosen to give his effort to this purpose. Thus he has used the powers within himself to set into motion the energy drawn into this function which shall, through the forms

expressed, flow to the purpose or to the individual intended. Essentially, he has set into motion a "cause"
which shall indeed produce its "effect" in accordance
with divine law.

When it is realized that every prayer brings into operation this process and function of the law, then one may
see that even "selfish" prayers may have a good purpose.
The extent of their power for good, however, may be
reduced substantially because of the conditions under
which they were given. For it logically follows that as the
quality of the purpose and promptings leading to the ut-
terance of the prayer is lessened, in the sense of optimum
for good, so, too, is the power transmitted lessened.

Every prayer carries some good with it. It is a form of
energy being transmitted from one to the other, and
energy is power which, in this instance, has been expressed in a form of prayer. Thus it can be said that
"even the worst of prayers" have some good in them; even
if it be but very little.

If the prayer is for healing, and that is primarily of
what we are speaking at this moment, the soul of the individual for whom you are praying definitely receives the
blessing of the power sent to it; and the soul is aware of it
and is indeed grateful for it.

But here, at this stage, other factors also enter in. Such
things as the karmic responsibilities then prevalent, the
attitudes, the thoughts and desires of the individual are
all some of the conditions which may go to determine
whether or not the healing which this soul has received
shall be permitted to become manifested in the physical
body it is wearing.

If you are suffering from an illness or physical discomfort and have received prayers from others, be grateful
for the blessings you have received from them; for they
have indeed reached your True Self. If the illness continues, or there are no other signs of help from the prayers,
such as a deep feeling of inner peace and strength, in

spite of outward physical discomfort, then, perhaps it is necessary for you to give thought to what we have said here.

Each person's present circumstance and condition is the outworking of what has gone before; this you know, or should know. Similarly, the illnesses and discomforts one may experience are because of this principle. But rather than allow this to lead to a negative form of acceptance of this condition, or allow this to limit one's incentive to grow and progress, we would suggest that these conditions be recognized as affording opportunities to learn, to grow, to gain the realizations they may offer for one to learn more about themselves.

Be willing, therefore, to bring whatever changes you can into your thinking and your attitudes that will allow you to profit most from any such experiences you may have. Thus you obtain a result which God's law has intended to bring about — you have learned, you have gained in and added to your understanding from the realization of the fact that you have brought into your life these "fruits" of your endeavors, whatever their quality, and thus are justly deserved.

This form of acceptance is a positive one. It is not negative or limiting unless you then merely make the acceptance without trying to do something to bring about changes designed to lead away from that level of living which produced them to a higher level of understanding.

Moreover, the power of the prayers flowing to you has contributed to this process of change just as does the light and the healing power which flows to each soul for whom you have prayed.

The other area that seems to involve your prayer is the desire for the realization of world peace.

Many minds in your land, and in other lands as well, are much concerned over the present status of the world. The tensions and conflicts and adverse economic conditions in many areas obviously give cause for serious concern over the human and governmental relationships which exist.

But we would remind you that in all times of stress and concern, of fear and of apprehension over such conditions as beset your planet at this time, it is necessary for you to consciously pull up short the actions of the human self and look deeper into yourself than that. Reap from the wisdom and the understanding that you can glean from your True Self.

The truth that is to be found within your Higher Self, the Christ of your being, shall bring you comfort and a strengthening of your faith; your concerns are lessened and the Peace of the Father shall dispel the fears and their negative persuasions.

To some, this suggestion may appear as serving only to treat one's individual problems and not as they may relate to the much larger problems prevailing throughout the world. But you must not lose sight of the fact and truth that as you invoke the Power and the Presence of God in your life, and bring It into active utilization in this way, you bring forth a very powerful force for good, both in your life and in the lives of many others. This action does much to still the troubled waters, the distraught emotions among men.

There must be those who shall serve as a "rock" among the many; who truly rely upon the wisdom and the love of the Father. And you must strive to be of this "service."

As you give acceptance to the principles which reveal that all things manifest and unmanifest are with purpose, and that all conditions and events and circumstances are caused by that which has gone before, and which served to be the cause of such effects—that all life functions and exists under these laws—you add to the strength of your convictions and resolve to serve the Father.

Thus you may more readily understand that the turmoil and unrest of this time has been earned and is the effect of what has gone before—principally the greed and self-seeking of men and of nations of men.

By his almost complete and utter reliance upon only the material substances and values of life and human reason, man has substituted his self-will and has sought to establish a self-hood apart from God. At best, such purposes and basis for living and life are only temporal, and are ideally suited as the birthplace of such conflict and tribulation as you witness today.

It is at times such as this, beloved brethren, that man may discover—or rediscover—the real Source of his strength, courage, and insight into the realities involved and of what his relationship to them may be.

You are certainly aware of those principles which deal with the teaching that God in His great love has created all things for good; that regardless of what comes out of the present difficulties and unrest upon the worldly plane, the outworking of God's laws is an immutable fact and governs the lives of all men; that in spite of man's inhumanity to man, all men are Children of God, and the Light, the Love and the Presence of God is within them —this Godly Presence ultimately to be expressed and to be manifested in all things by you and by them.

Perhaps it is extremely difficult to see how any good may come from what is presently visible in these relationships existent. But the divine truths underlying all things are of infinite power and strength, reaching far beyond human concepts and understanding, and sooner or later manifest this fact. The real test for you is your willingness and ability to rely upon this assurance and your faith which supports it. It is for you to hold to this truth with all the fervor and faith you can muster. And to the extent that you do this, you shall find yourself being carried through these and other difficult times freed from the burdens they would place upon you.

We would suggest, however, that there is yet an essential counterpart to this requirement. That is, the need for you to give full support towards practicing the commandment set forth by the Master: To love your neighbor as yourself; to do unto him as you would have him do unto you. For unless and until this is the true motivation of all your relationships with your fellow man, they shall be very shallow and of little strength; they shall not withstand the tests of stress and conflict which the human nature of man inevitably introduces into such relationships.

You have had opportunity to observe that in many areas where these problems lie, much of what is being done is being carried out in the name of religion. We do not pass judgment upon this practice, nor should you do so either. We point out, however, that many of such practices are contrary to the principles of goodwill which ordinarily one would expect to see flowing from the light of God's love. The test of "By their fruits ye shall know them" has application to the actions of all men, whatever may be their religious belief or pursuit.

Divine truth with its power and spirit for good is found to be the thrust of the Ancient Wisdoms and all its Progeny, even though man has always found ways to misinterpret it. But this has not destroyed the truth which awaits manifestation through whatever means may ultimately be provided for the outworking of God's law.

It is essential that you devote time and energy to the giving of prayer and thoughts of love to all peoples in all areas of the world. It matters not which "side" of any controversy they may represent. And do this *KNOWING* that God's love and His law shall indeed prevail.

The power of love given selflessly unto others is so very great. Use it! Send it forth! Let it radiate from your hearts unfettered and filled with all the feeling you can muster of goodwill.

Withhold judgment and condemnation of any kind, even though this may be difficult to do. Remember the Master's words: "Father, forgive them; for they know not what they do." Continuously remind yourself of the fact that all men are indeed Sons of God as are you. Hold the light of this truth ever in your consciousness.

As you actively practice principles of love, you gain in your ability to be of service unto others and as a "Light Bearer." For as your service becomes more pure, and more active its effectiveness increases more rapidly. Indeed, this functions much as an arithmetical progression.

Chapter 13

POWER OF LOVE

Love is the essence of your life. Love is the substance of all things. God is love. What greater power, what greater essence of being, what greater motivation in life would there be for you or anyone else, than to be and to give love?

How frequently have you used the word "Love" and, in using it, given any thought at all to the fullness and the greatness of the power that it expresses, denotes and defines?

It is unfortunate that your society has made the use of this term as it has to where, for many people, it has grown to have little meaning. Also, for many it is used only in the sense of denoting sensual activities and relationships. Obviously, this detracts and takes from the power it is really meant to carry and to give.

We do not, however, mean to say that this has in any way actually taken from the power of love—true divine love—for this is not the case at all. It is the blockage that is created through these human concepts and human usages which brings about a loss of value in its use. To the masses it has become a trivial expression of misdirected meaning.

Nevertheless, we would ask you this: How much thought, if any, have you given to the use being made of this word? What does "love" mean to you? When you speak this word, or otherwise use it, do you consciously

111

invoke the God Power and Presence through it? When you invoke God's Love in a wish to, or a blessing upon your fellow man, do you give any thought to what you are giving him, of what you are sending out?

We do not ask these questions as any form of test or for any ulterior purpose. To the contrary, we pose them that you would pause to think upon this, not for just this moment, but frequently; that you would find it extremely important to give much thought and contemplation to this beautiful term: Love.

Indeed, as the Beloved John so aptly and correctly wrote: "God is love." It is fitting that all men give much thought to this and examine their concepts and ideas concerning it. We would suggest that you do this regularly, and that you give particular attention to your attitudes and the nature of your thoughts and purposes at those times when you are using and expressing this powerful word: Love.

As you do this, you shall find and observe that your present ideas and understanding concerning it, and your usages of it, shall change considerably from what they are, and they likely shall continue to undergo change.

Each day in your life brings with it something new. It may not seem as such or, perhaps, the changes may not be noticeable, especially it you have long dwelled upon negative thoughts and ideas. But as you strive to carry out what you take to be God's will in your life, each step brings you to new ground. Correspondingly, your ideas, concepts and understanding, of necessity, shall also move onto new ground.

This is life. This is the evolvement, development and unfoldment you have heard and read so much about. Thus you must indeed have concern for the souls who do not permit or allow this to happen in their lives. Thus you may understand why we suggest you do all you can to encourage change and growth and to discourage stagnation and negativism in both yourself and in others.

"Love ye one another as I have loved you." So teaches the Beloved Master, Jesus. And so do we also teach this divine principle, dear brethren. Truly strive to fulfill this profoundly essential principle of Brotherhood in your life—and in your daily living—that this law may be fulfilled.

The practice of giving of the Father's love to one another extends to all planes of life. Indeed great is our love for you. Always are we at your side, moving with you along the path you follow, giving you our love and our guidance as best we can.

And so, too, should you extend your love, your help and your care to those about you. For this provides a means for the outworking and expression of the Father's Presence and Power both in you and in your fellow man.

We would also suggest that for a time you endeavor to make guarded use of the word, Love. That is, that you use it *ONLY* to express consciously the Power and Presence of the Father-Mother God. Whatever the circumstances or the situation, carefully restrict your thoughts and the expression of this term to the sole purpose of channeling God's love and grace. Consciously recognize that when you do this, you are manifesting and expressing powers God has entrusted to your care and use. Indeed, "The Father that dwelleth in me, he doeth the works."

To the degree that you carry out this practice, you increase measurably the strength and quality of the power of the love you thus express and send forth. Remember what was written concerning the Word. "The Word was with God, and the Word was God."

Herein we have given you a teaching of much depth. Think carefully upon these things, meditate upon them. And resolve that you shall indeed strive always to serve as an instrument of the Father's love—living it, giving it, and *BEING IT*. A tremendous responsibility this, but such a gracious and beautiful one, producing naught but blessings and happiness and much joy. So why tarry? USE THE POWER OF GOD—USE AND GIVE OF HIS LOVE TO ALL MEN!

The Master Jesus' actions—His going among the people, His teachings and His demonstration of the principle of love—should be carefully studied. Bear in mind that the teachings and demonstrations given by Jesus were not intended only for the incarnate of that time, but, indeed, are intended for you, our dear incarnate brethren, and for all who would hear them and take them into their understanding and consciousness.

Much has been said as to the significances which are to be drawn from those events. Indeed, substantial differences in interpretations and meanings have been ascribed to them. It is our view, however, that it is the responsibility and the privilege of each one, individually, to make his own determination and judgment as to which significance and meaning he shall accept.

Obviously, it is our purpose to give guidance and suggestions as best we can that will assist you in traveling your path to understanding, wisdom and spiritual unfoldment. Even so, it is your decision as to whether or not you would wish to use anything we give you. For this is a part of your "growing up." This also is why we never seek to force our teaching upon you. This follows the form with which the Master Jesus brought forward His teachings. Proceeding upon this basis, we would give you a few thoughts which you may wish to consider.

We would suggest the following: Using the power of your minds, take yourself back to the time that Jesus was present upon Earth giving these teachings. Now, being as objective as you possibly can be, try to recognize the variance in attitudes which must have existed in the minds and hearts of those who sought to follow after Jesus, from those who sought to uphold the principles, doctrines, dogma and rituals of the church of that day. Obviously, there was a conflict between them.

When viewed from the position of the leaders of the church who sought to uphold their views of the law of Moses, the activities and the teachings of the young rabbi, Jesus, were very much a problem for them. And, if you are able to hold such an objective point of view, you can more readily understand why there would be such conflict and the feeling in the "church" that Jesus and His disciples were guilty of insurrection.

Indeed, we would say that if you look to your own day, you find that while you have great freedom of worship and expression, the majority of the churches and formal religions of your time ridicule what you believe, including the means by which you receive of our teachings. Frequently, you find yourself accused of being engaged in "the devil's work."

Yet, in your heart, you know that you are right in what you do and that you are on the right path, chosen because it brings you the light and understanding you have long sought after. Just as the disciples and followers of Jesus sought after spiritual truth and greater realization of their purpose in life, so, too, do you seek after these things.

The point we seek to make by this, dear brethren, is the fact that you are, in many respects, challenged as much today by those who would ridicule you and condemn you for the form of your spiritual endeavor as were your ancestors. But, remember, the Master forewarned that such would be the case.

But also remember that all the strength, all the power, and all the courage you need to hold strong in your faith, and to carry you forward along the path you follow, is already yours—you have it within you.

So you are encouraged not to avoid entering into your own gardens of Gethsemane, if this need be. Sometimes the burdens that come from such experiences are very heavy and you may find yourself filled with great sorrow, knowing not where to turn nor where to go. When this occurs, do as the Master has done: Turn within and find there the power of the Father's Presence and Love.

Thus, you find the strength that the Master Jesus found. You find the power to resist the temptations which would have you turn away from your quest after truth and your striving to bring this truth forth as the expression of your life.

Have no fear. Replace fear with the power of God's love. Fear is the fruit of darkness. Love is the fruit of light, the light within, the light which becomes more radiant as you express your divine essence.

In your Earth life, you are faced with problems of varying degree but each one is open to solution and resolution. But their solution will not come about unless, and until, you confront them and work with them. Without fail, each of you can find within yourself the answers to your problems, but you must go there to find them. For there you shall find God, and with God all things are possible.

Thus you receive of the fruits of the Father's love and enter in His kingdom and fulfill your responsibility as a laborer in His vineyard, and join in the harvest of His love.

Meditate upon the words of the Master Jesus. Read them many times over and ponder on the truths they give. If you are led to other spiritual and inspirational writings that appeal to you, read and study them, for they shall, no doubt, increase your knowledge and ability of discerning that which is of greatest value to your spiritual pursuits.

Continue joyfully upon your quest for truth. Whenever you find new meaning and realization of truth, make it a part of your life. Live it and express it as a part of your consciousness and being. Thus are you filled with joy and enabled to more fully release the light of the Christ which dwells within your heart.

Thus, dear ones, we again place before you certain principles which are of paramount importance to your spiritual well-being, especially at this time and stage of your life. To some of you, it may seem that we have said nothing new, and, in a sense, this may be true. However, we would remind you that we never place before you anything that is not needed.

Whether or not these teachings are used and followed is your decision. This, of course, is true in all areas of truth and life. Each one is responsible for his own debts and reaps his own rewards.

Ultimately the perfection of the Christ, which already is yours, shall become manifest in you and your life. But until this Glory of Fulfillment is reached, you must find solace, comfort and strength in the realizations attained through taking these steps one at a time as best as you can. Each of you has found much joy, and your enthusiasm has been renewed, from the revelations you have received. Thus you move forward upon the Path, the Path founded upon the Father's Love.

Chapter 14

SETTING UP A PRAYER HEALING GROUP

The light of the stars radiates the power of their essence. The light of your hearts radiates the power of their essence. Indeed, all things, all creatures, have light. For the light, my beloved, is the Spirit. It is the life, it is the BE-ING that has been given unto it; that which it has received from and of the Father.

EXCEPT for a few minor changes, the format for the Prayer Healing Service is the same that has been used by the groups formed under the auspices of Azrael's work for nearly 40 years. We think it presents a very inspirational and powerful means of serving our fellow man. While it is designed to be used by groups, it may be used by any individual who wishes to have some form of prayer service to follow. You may meet as a group or have your individual Service on any day or hour convenient to you. But we would suggest that you try to maintain a regular time for having this Service, as this helps add to the power of your work.

The format given below is self-explanatory, however, we would add this additional information:

(1) The "sacred breaths" are basically a form of breathing exercise suggested by Azrael. We slow down our breathing by inhaling slowly, filling our lungs completely, holding the breath for a short interval, then exhaling slowly. It is helpful to time each of these steps, as

118

if each one was a side to a triangle; the breathing in, the holding, and the breathing out, each of equal length. Repeat this cycle seven times. And, as you do so, envision the inhalation of the beautiful healing White Light of God's Love permeating every atom of your being, and as you exhale, you send this blessing of Love and healing out to every soul in the universe as a gift from God.

(2) We use the Gospel of John solely as the source of our Scriptural reading. Beginning with the first chapter, we divide the Gospel into equal segments of reasonable length and read a segment for each Service, continuing to the end of the Gospel at which time we start back at the beginning chapter.

(3) The reading from Azrael's teachings may be a portion selected from this book, or from The New Angelus.

(4) The prayers are read in the segments as indicated and by each one in the group taking his regular turn. The groups generally seat themselves in a circle and all readings are carried on clockwise around the circle. If alone, you may wish to read all of the prayers, in fact, to go through the entire Service, or at least so much of it as your inner guidance may direct you to read.

We invite you to participate in this work, for you shall find it a tremendously rewarding experience from the inner peace alone that it gives, much less the many other blessings which flow from a selfless devotion to this service for others.

PHILIP

Beloved brethren, we frequently speak upon the wonderful service of prayer. Indeed, throughout this book you shall find statements concerning the great power you have when you engage in this practice. And especially is this true when you engage in the prayer healing work we have sponsored and suggested. We therefore encourage you to follow this practice as much as you possibly can, using the Service we have suggested, if you wish. But whether you serve as a member of a group, or individually, know that you serve as a channel and instrument for the Father's Healing Grace to do its work specifically in this fashion. We bless you in your endeavor, for you are truly blessed through participating in this work. And now follows the Prayer Healing Service in the format we have suggested.

PRAYER, MEDITATION AND HEALING SERVICE

Reverence of the highest is the keynote of our service, consequently this hour is set apart wholly for prayer, meditation and healing. May we realize that we are not alone, but that those assigned by the Great White Brotherhood are with us, aiding us, helping our souls to unfold and grow in God during the service we render to the Brotherhood on High, and to the Master thereof, Jesus the Christ.

⊕

We open by making the Sign of the Cross, and repeating aloud: "IN THE NAME OF THE FATHER, THE SON, AND THE HOLY SPIRIT. AMEN."

Prayer.

Each takes seven Sacred Breaths in order to raise his vibrations and link in with the Higher Vibrations of the Brotherhood.

Scripture reading by the one designated.

The reading of the chosen portion of the teachings of the Great White Brotherhood as given by Azrael.

Meditation period.

Offering of prayers:

A PRAYER FOR ALL MANKIND

DEAR GOD, WE PRAY:

For the sorrowing who mourn lost ones. May they realize

the truth of life, that there is NO death; that their loved ones live on as they themselves will live on, endlessly.

For the sick and suffering, in home and hospital, and for those struck down on the waysides of the world. May they have divine release from pain, and may that harmony come unto them which heals disease.

For the sick in mind, in mental homes and hospitals and in private homes. May they be lifted into the light of understanding and mental health.

For those in jails, in prisons and all places of confinement. May enlightenment come to them while their walks of life are so circumscribed.

For the disquieted souls of men, on Earth and in the astral realms. Bring them into Thy peace, oh God. May they learn the KEY to Thy peace: LOVING, SELFLESS SERVICE.

For the helpless, the poor, the hungry, the shelterless. Open our hearts, the hearts of their Earth brethren, that their needs may be supplied.

For the lonely, the heart-hungry, those away from home and loved ones. May they find the divine Companion within, the Christ, to comfort them.

For the Youth of all nations. May there be a new environment created for them, that they may live in purity of thought, purity of word, and purity of deed, in Thee.

For those in the sunset of life. May their "going home" be easy and painless, as Thou preparest them now, oh God, for service in the World of Light above.

For all humanity, from the North Pole to the South Pole, and all around the Earth. May a universal brotherhood become their guiding motive, so that PEACE may be in all the world.

For Thine Angels, Thy Saints and Martyrs, Thy Holy Ones. May the way open that Thy Light shining through them may reach out and quicken every soul to realize the eternal truth and beauty of Brotherhood between all Realms of Being.

For the fighting forces of every race and nation, which we sincerely hope will soon no longer be needed. Illumine their leaders; open their eyes to the truth which will cause wars to cease forever—the truth that ALL MEN are brothers!

For those who have been released from Earth's cares and lessons. May a peace be with them, and a deeper understanding of life's true purpose and meaning come to them as they now study in the Halls of Learning beyond the grave.

For the leaders of each and every race and nation. May each heart and mind open to the truth of ETERNAL BROTHERHOOD. May the leaders help to open the way under Thy Guidance, beloved Father-Mother of us all, so that Brotherhood may come into *all* the Earth.

We pray that all of the world may be stirred to pray for the coming of PEACE, for the cessation forever of war between nations and races, between factions and individuals, so that Thy Kingdom may truly come on Earth as it is in Heaven.

Amen.

PRAYER FOR LOVE AND BROTHERHOOD

Infinite Almighty God, our Father, we lift our hearts and minds in prayer for our brethren of every race and nation, of every color and every creed, and for the creedless, and we pray that there may be peace in and understanding among all nations, now and forever more.

We pray for our animal brethren, who give us love and affection when we give them opportunity to do so, and we pray for all animals in all the world, and for all life, that it, too, may evolve as we hope to evolve to the highest possible for us.

We pray that the Spirit of Christ, of love and brotherhood, may become ever more living within our hearts, and within the hearts and minds of every man, woman and child on Earth, and in those realms beyond where the Light is yet dim. We pray deeply also for those in the realms where darkness yet reigns, praying that Light may break there, and everywhere.

Amen.

THE HEALING MINISTRY

The Healing Ministry is begun with the following prayer:

"Lord Christ, Thou Who art the Master Healer, we bring before Thee these our loved ones, friends and relatives, and the names of those we have been given as in need, knowing that even as we speak these names Thy Light within them is quickened. May their minds, hearts and bodies, and their circumstances, become receptive to Thy Healing Rays, so that peace and harmony may come to them as needed lessons on life's pathway are learned and understood."

(Now each one in turn speaks aloud the names of those you offer up for healing of body, mind, soul or circumstance. *SPEAK THE NAMES LOUDLY ENOUGH FOR ALL TO HEAR! AND PAUSE A BRIEF MOMENT IN BETWEEN EACH NAME SPOKEN!* The reason for speaking the names aloud and distinctly is so each one present may also take a part in "lifting them up" in thought and prayer as you speak their names; indeed, it is requested that each one repeat each name silently within his own mind and concentrate on sending healing to them at that moment. It is helpful also to "picture each person in your mind's eye" as healed and in the state of being as prayed for.)

PRAISE AND THANKSGIVING

When there are no more names to be lifted in prayer for healing, it is fitting that the leader lift his or her voice in praise and thanksgiving in gratitude for the blessings received.

THE LORD'S PRAYER

This prayer is recited by all present using the word "debts" instead of "trespasses" and "*Leave* us not *when* in temptation" in place of "*Lead* us not *into* temptation:" as the more correct translation of the phrase involved. And it is suggested that the group join hands during the speaking of the prayer and thus experience the added sense of oneness and spiritual power present within each one and in your midst.

CLOSING PRAYERS
(In Unison)

"Oh Master of the Great White Lodge,
Lord of all the religions of the world,
Thou comest again to the world that needs Thee
To help the nations that are longing for Thy Presence.
"Thou speakest the word of Peace
Which shall cause the peoples to cease their warring;
Thou speakest the word of Brotherhood,
Which shall make all quarreling classes and castes to
    know themselves as one in Thee.
"Thou comest in the Might of Thy Love;
Thou comest in the splendor of Thy Power to bless the
    world which is longing for Thy Coming,
Thou Who art the Teacher alike of angels and of men.
                      Amen."

"We close this Chain of Prayer, which we pray may encircle the world, in the Name of the Father, the Son, and the Holy Spirit, Amen. May the memory of this hour sustain and enrich your life until we meet again."

⊕

This Prayer Healing Service, and its exercises, practices and techniques, if you will, can be helpful in developing your powers of concentration and the direction of your power of thought and related aspects of this phenomenon. It is our sincere hope, however, that you shall use these practices only because of motivations that are based upon the desire to be of service to your fellow man, and selflessly so. Indeed, we would say that any other motivation should not be honored, the reason for this is obvious. We would also suggest that you guard against letting the content of this Service become a matter of rote. Consciously think upon the meaning of the prayers as they are read, realizing that there also are esoteric meanings and significances being used and expressed and that this is a service of divine order that you are carrying out.

You are not seeking to build up your powers, or your channelship of such power, for the sake of power. Rather, you strive to enlarge upon your capacity to serve and to be of service. And this is the real key to the solid and beautiful spiritual unfoldment and growth you aspire to.

We take much joy in observing you use these forms of service and finding them as useful tools in your labor of love in the Father's kingdom in which you serve.

Chapter 15

GUIDANCE ON USING THE BLESSED GIFTS OF:
The Power of Thought; The Power of Prayer;
and The Power of Love

Chart your path and your direction of travel accordingly, following carefully and well the signposts placed along the way, and you shall reach your destination more surely and more quickly and in the joy of the blessings of the Father, which are so abundantly given unto you.

THE POWER OF THOUGHT

THE thoughts which flow from your minds are varied, but, at this moment, as we meet together, they dwell mainly upon spiritual matters, upon spiritual wishes and thoughts of love and thanksgiving. For some, your interest is in your loved ones, both incarnate and discarnate. Others are concerned with their own endeavors and of their efforts with those with whom they are associated and work.

We make note of these observations for several purposes, the more important of which, however, has to do with drawing your attention once again to the power of thought, to the power of your minds.

The expressions we previously have made concerning the creative power of thought have not been simple, idle expressions given only in passing, but have been designed to assist you in reaching a fuller understanding of the axiomatic nature of this truth. Indeed, the area of thought

126

power and thought forms, and the effects flowing from them, is such as to require a student of truth to lend more than passing interest to them.

Your thoughts create that on which you think. The goals you bring from your mind and fix and hold in your thoughts are the goals which you shall reach, just as you attain those circumstances and conditions you most persistently hold in your thoughts.

It is not our purpose at this time to reiterate any further on the aspects of this profound principle, except to speak briefly upon the quality of thoughts as they pertain to the distinction between those which are of a positive nature and those which are negative.

You, and you alone, hold the power to control the form your thoughts shall take, this power being a part of the independent, yet divinely granted and endowed, power of will and choice. This, of course, includes the power to change and to transmute the quality and form of your thoughts and also of the direction they are meant to take.

When we speak of thoughts that are positive in nature, we are referring principally to those which are spiritually uplifting and of a selfless nature, filled with love and kindness, and supported by attitudes of tolerance and forbearance to the adverse thoughts and actions directed towards you by others. Obviously, mental activities motivated by purposes that would hold to attitudes of this nature are beneficent and valuable to the one employing them.

On the other hand, the thoughts flowing from a negatively oriented mind or attitude and purpose are destructive and harmful, not only to the one who sends them forth, but also to the environment into which they are released and to those within that environment.

If perchance you are not fully convinced of the differing effects the form of your thoughts may have upon you, we suggest you conduct an experiment upon yourself.

For a fixed period of time purposefully and deliberately think only negative thoughts. You may find this difficult to do because of your commitment to truth, but, if necessary, force yourself to do this. And, as you are able to do this, you shall soon find yourself experiencing an adverse feeling leading you into an attitude and sense of self-pity, sadness, sorrow, and even into a depression if practiced long enough. Indeed, you may very well experience a generally strong feeling of negativity.

Having had a taste of the fruits of this form and quality of thought, consciously reverse the direction of your thoughts to a positive nature. Now, as you concentrate upon this opposite direction of thinking, you shall find a different force entering into your life. You are likely to sense a feeling of being lifted up, as from darkness into light, with the release of a great heaviness and burdensome weight that the negative thoughts and thought forms had placed upon you and about you.

To carry this experiment further, we would suggest the following: Tomorrow morning, after having risen from your night's rest, completed your meditation, and entered into your usual morning's activities, pause for a moment and quickly take an inventory of the quality of your thoughts up to that point. Have they been positive, or have they been negative?

If you have been thinking principally negative thoughts, either about yourself or about others, then we would say your day has gotten off to a bad start and many of your actions, and the effects ensuing, shall reflect that form of vibration. If you find this to be the case, quickly set about changing the negative thoughts into positive ones. Lest you take this form of action, you profit little from what we have given you.

Perhaps this form of thinking flows from old habits that have not been fully broken and released from your consciousness and way of doing things. If you are continuing to entertain negative thoughts when you would rather not do so, then it would be wise to make it a persistent practice to follow some form of exercise which shall consciously direct your mind away from that habit of thought into a new channel of positive thinking. Well chosen affirmations and affirmative prayers directed to this purpose are helpful and effective. A continuing conscious awareness of the nature of your thoughts can also be an effective way of disciplining yourself and your mind in this regard.

But, here again, you must necessarily observe that it must be *you* who exercises both the will and the power to bring about this change. As you desire such change, and then affirmatively seek to bring it about, the good fruits of your decision and endeavor shall become manifest in your life. This is the law.

You must realize, however, that while efforts which are blessed and energized with positive thought and attitude bring forth good fruit, their fruitage may not serve as a panacea for all your problems. Even so, with such a positive attitude and purpose, your ability to face and to meet the problems and challenges of your life is enhanced manifold.

Be wise in your thoughts and thus in the use of the holy power which lies within you, for, through the power of positive thought and action, dedicated to godly purpose and to the fulfillment of God's will, you gain an ever-increasing realization of your relationship with God and of the fruits this relationship is meant to bring to you.

One of the more effective ways to transform negative thoughts to positive ones is through the use of the Brotherhood Prayer set forth below. It may be repeated as an affirmation and used to build a powerful positive thought that when released helps to influence your direction to the inevitable state of true brotherhood.

A BROTHERHOOD PRAYER

Our Father, Thy servants present themselves before Thee being duly prepared, waiting Thy com-

mands. We remember that with Thy Wisdom in our hearts, Thy Beauty in our vision, and Thy Will in our hands, we may go forward to complete Thy Work in Thy Name, to Thine honour and glory. So may it be!

THE POWER OF PRAYER

A number of you regularly meet to give prayers for healing, to serve as instruments and channels for God's healing grace and love, so it may flow unto those for whom you pray and to whom you give thoughts of love. We do not repeat what we have earlier stated concerning this work, except to remind you of the immense power given to you which flows through you when you give yourself to this practice.

And this phenomenon does not only occur when you are joined together in a regular Prayer Healing Service but also in the privacy of your home, in your heart—"into thy closet," as the Master has said—for what you do there also serves to do a good work.

It is wise to be diligent in your prayer work, for this, indeed, is a demonstration of love. The prayer of a saint, with which you are familiar, asked to be made an instrument of the Father's peace; so also may you pray. For as you ask, you shall certainly receive, and, as you ask to be used as an instrument of God's peace, you are so used. And your endeavor need not only be directed to the conflicts between nations and races of people, but to the personal relationships within your own environment, wherever you may be.

So many of the leaders of people speak of peace, and, perhaps, sincerely want peace, but they refuse to consider their need to give up any position of authority or power they may hold over others casting them into a position of inequality, suppressive of their neighbor's rights. The Beloved Master has given to these, and to all men, a perfect "test" for determining the validity of their relationships with all others, saying: "Whatsoever ye would that men should do to you, do ye even so to them." Unfortunately, this law, which is found within the tenets of all religions and beliefs, is often forgotten and overlooked in the formulation of political policies.

Therefore, it is all the more important that you invite the power of love, which does indeed bring peace and harmony, to flow fully and abundantly from you and through you unto all men. Although the effectiveness of your efforts may not immediately become visible or externalized in the affairs of your fellow man—perhaps even appearing to have become lost in the darkness which surrounds so many—know that the light of the love which you have sent forth does indeed penetrate and transmute the darkness to which it reaches.

Remember, beloved brethren, no act of love, of kindness, of good, is ever lost or wasted; its good work is fulfilled, perhaps only upon the inner planes for the time being, but know that it truly is the power of God, the power of His love, which doeth the good works; and thus it never fails.

Take of the Father's love, experience the joy that it brings and gives to you to give unto others. Be examples of what a glorious and beneficent force and power this is and can be, and others will soon want to have what you have. Thus you are enabled to give them the gift of your love in even greater abundance and, having done this, you find that you have received even more than you had before. This is the functioning of God's love, and the source of that peace which surpasseth all understanding. May you find this peace now!

All of life has its purpose indeed. All of life is a beautiful outworking of the Father's law and His love. This truth can be the source of everlasting joy in your heart. Your prayers shall do much towards obtaining fulfillment of that goal.

Very often you may find yourself needing a certain prayer that will help you "tune in" so that you may feel your prayers are more effective. Though the sincerity in your heart and the spirit of selfless love are the true measure of the effectiveness of your prayers, we give you a prayer that you may wish to use to send with your healing prayers to others. This prayer was given many years ago by our beloved brother, White Eagle, to the devoted followers of his teachings, the members of The White Eagle Lodge of England. We know that you shall find it most effective and helpful. It is as follows:

> *In the holy name of Christ, by the Christ Light in the hearts of men, we call upon the great Angels of Christ, we feel their presence and their power. We attune ourselves to the prayers of all men of goodwill.*
>
> *Being thus prepared and ready before God— With all the will of our minds, with all the love of our deepest heart, WE SEND FORTH THE LIGHT.*
>
> *We send it forth as a great Star of Light, a Star of Love, a blazing Star, withstanding, overcoming all evil, triumphant over death, a star of the Christ Light.*
>
> *BY ALL THE POWER OF CHRIST WITHIN, WE SEND FORTH THE LIGHT.*

THE POWER OF LOVE

The thoughts you hold in your minds, the desires you hold in your hearts, all go to build, for us and for yourselves, a beautiful temple: a temple of light, radiant to the degree of the love you bring into it. And this, as you know, dearly beloved brethren, controls and determines how bright and how beautiful it may be.

The question comes to your mind, and to the minds of many others, of why it is that we speak so frequently upon this principle of love, why do so many of our messages treat upon this principle.

Our answer must be, and always shall be: We seek to fulfill the teachings of the Master Jesus, to bring to your hearts, to your understanding the dire necessity which exists in the divine plan that you, indeed, all men, must come to manifest fully the principle of brotherhood, of peace and goodwill to all men.

These are not meant to be idle words or expressions of encouragement only. No, these are statements of principle and of truth. Indeed, do you not recall the words of the Master wherein he expressed these as commandments?

Knowledge, increased awareness, lifting of consciousness, all these aspects of life and growth in life to which all seekers after truth aspire, are good and are necessary. But you must never allow yourself to forget that the principle of love made manifest in your life upon a day to day, moment to moment, basis is also necessary. Without love, all else is as nothing!

So it is our purpose and our mission to teach love. And, as you learn from us, you also serve to teach others as you practice these principles of selflessness and giving of self. Indeed, through this process, we all are drawn closer together and are covered by the Light of the Christ which radiates both from without and from within the beings of each one. This is the light of love, the power of the universe, the form of cosmic energy about which so much has been both written and spoken, yet about which so many really know so little.

We do not say this critically. We state only fact. And it is only through the assimilation of fact and truth that you grow, and unfold the true nature of your beings. It is important to us that you, dearly beloved brethren, make yourselves better able to serve as channels for this power to flow through, and for us to work through; indeed, for the Christ to work through, that God's will may be made manifest among all men.

We, therefore, humbly express our gratitude to you, for without you, without your help, we would, perhaps, find it difficult to reach others, especially those we are able to reach through you.

Yes, dear brethren, you are our arms, our hands, our feet. You serve as the instruments by which the peace of God may reach others. Do not ever feel that you are standing at the outer limits looking in. Rather, consider yourselves as being in the center, looking out to those who would come to join with you.

Your work must go on, and, by and through the Grace of the Father-Mother God, it shall go on. And, to the extent that each of you may practice the principles of love and brotherhood, you shall find your work to be enhanced and blessed.

We take this opportunity to join in closer communion with you and to allow you to join closer with your brethren and, all together, with the Father. To do this, we ask you to use the power of your mind, of your heart and your soul, and create within your mind's eye a temple: a temple of love, of light. Make this temple into the most beautiful structure of pure white light you can possibly comprehend it to be.

Now, let us all together, hand in hand, enter in. As we become enfolded in the beauty and the warmth of the light all about us, we recognize the light as being the light of the Christ Love, the Christ Presence which permeates us and all that is about us.

In the center of the temple there is a beautiful altar, also of pure white substance, and upon it have been placed the symbols of the bread and the wine. We are invited to approach the altar and receive of the bread and the wine.

But, first, we pause for a moment and place ourselves into a deep state of reverence and gratitude, for truly we know that we are in the Presence of the Christ. May you sense this blessing and joyfully give appropriate thought and recognition to it.

Now, we are handed the bread, and the voice of the Christ, having given thanks unto the Father, bids us, "Take and eat, this is the symbol of my Cosmic Body given unto you." And in like manner, we are handed the cup and told, "Take ye and drink of it, this is the symbol of my Cosmic Spirit given unto you." Immediately, we feel the added blessing of this form of communion with the Christ, quickening even more the power of His Presence within us.

And, having been so blessed, we give thanks unto the Father, and slowly withdraw from the altar and the temple, returning to our respective levels of present consciousness and being.

Each of you shall have received abundantly from this experience in the knowing that each one is indeed a Child of God, a Child of the Father Who loves us more deeply and dearly than it is possible for us to understand. Thus, we do indeed take of these blessings with great joy and thanksgiving. Yet, all the while, we must ever remain aware of the responsibilities which flow from and are a part of this relationship with the Father: That we must truly demonstrate that which we are — Love!

Let your love manifest in the supreme glory that it is, and all else that is good and of the light shall come unto you and be given unto you. This, beloved brethren, is the promise of the Christ!

We believe it appropriate to end this section with the prayer we call our "Prayer to the Spirit of Love."

SPIRIT OF LOVE, *our Father: May our beloved brethren of Earth receive Thy blessings in the light of Thy Son, Divine Love. We are all brethren in the same spirit, both on Earth and with those who have passed beyond the veil. We look to Thee for guidance and pray that the gentle spirit of Jesus the Christ may take possession of us all. May inspiration ever renewed from day to day bring wisdom and understanding so that unity among Thy Children may*

*bring forth the fruits of perfect harmony and peace
in their hearts and in their lives.*

*Grant, we pray Thee, peace on Earth and good-
will to men, and may courage and faith walk hand
in hand to stimulate afresh all those who are working for brotherhood in Thy world.*

Amen.

Chapter 16

SEEKING AND PRACTICING
THE DIVINE PRESENCE

Our Father, which art in heaven, O Holy Divine Presence, may each of these, our dear brethren, become fully conscious and aware of Thy Presence and be lifted up and be more fully opened to the light of Thy Love, and thus be purified and blessed and given deeper insight into all things that flow from Thee.

Blessed be Thy Holy Presence, Thy Love, and Thy Light, O Father. In the name of Thy Son, the Christ, we pray.

Amen.

WE BEGIN with a question. It is this: Have you truly sought to find the Divine Presence within yourself? Let your answer be made within the silence of your heart, and only after much thought, contemplation and prayerful self-examination. If you have not given much attention to the principle involved in this inquiry do not assume that you are alone in this respect, for there are a multitude of souls who have not concerned themselves with this matter.

Your quest for spiritual unfoldment, and the corresponding growth towards the realization in your life of the brilliance and the glory of the Christ Star that such unfoldment brings, is affected substantially by the principle involved. There also lies within this principle, and your working with it, one of the deeper mysteries. But what is involved is no easy task.

First, there is the need for you to gain in your general understanding of the principle itself. Much has been said and written about it by those who know and understand what is involved and intended to be brought into your consciousness, and by those who do not really understand, but believe that they do. We think it is important for you to remember that frequently truth lies hidden or buried in simple statements and the words used in them. Indeed, this is so even with many of the statements we have used throughout the years we have given our teachings. Because of the simplicity of expression we so frequently use in the form of our statements, there are those who take the view that our teachings are "not high enough" for them, and they go elsewhere seeking after ideas and philosophies expressed in more complex and sophisticated fashion. But after a time of experimenting with that work and wading through all their "complexities and sophistications" they realize that the basic ideas and principles being taught by the Master, through us, are indeed essential and must be learned *and lived,* and are the substantive truths they were seeking in the first place.

We would make it clear, however, that we do not criticize anyone for the path they select or choose to follow. Indeed, as we frequently point out: No effort expended in quest of truth and spiritual enlightenment is wasted effort. For each effort leads ultimately to the right end. Even the grossly wrong ones serve a good purpose. Once their inadequacies are found out, they are left for something more valuable. And thus the seeker has profited from his experience. If not, then he will go through similar experiences repeatedly until he does learn better. And when he finally gains the wisdom such experiences offer, he is ready to enter upon other more productive endeavors.

There are many techniques and practices one can follow and use in quest of spiritual unfoldment. However, the Ancient Wisdom teaches that meditation is the superior practice and is unsurpassed in its value as a technique for such purpose. Admittedly, there are myriad suggestions one may receive from as many sources as to how to meditate.

At this point, we do not enter into any discussion on meditation techniques, except to say that the important thing is for you to choose some form of meditation practices that you feel comfortable with, and then use it regularly. If you do not feel good about the technique you are now using, then change to some other. Find a way that does gain the approval of your Inner Self, and then *use it!* We do suggest that you meditate regularly every day. In time, you shall reap a beautiful and bountiful harvest from your efforts.

The fact remains, and paradoxically so, that the seeker after spiritual truth is also in quest of a better understanding of himself, his *real Self,* and of what relationship that Self may have with God. Thus, he finds that regardless of where his search may take him, he ultimately is led back to where he began — to himself. Remember what the Master teaches about this: "The kingdom of God is within you."

Moreover, the realization of the kingdom of God within "cometh not with observation," but from recognition and obedience to His law, which the Beloved Master has clearly defined and stated in the form of the "Commandments of Love." These give you the direction in which you are to move. "Love the Lord thy God, with all your heart and with all your soul and with all your mind, and love your neighbor as yourself." And when you have accomplished this, you shall find that you have also accomplished your purposes in this life and shall have indeed found the "Divine Presence within."

Lest you would be discouraged by your progress toward this heavenly goal, we would remind you of what has been demonstrated to you many times over: That by the mere extension of your desire and effort in this direction, you immediately invoke the beautiful and powerful Grace of the Father which brings Its blessings into your life; blessings, which obviously have not yet been earned nor deserved, but which, nevertheless, are abundant in both number and in scope.

My beloved brethren, the Father's love is so great, so all encompassing, magnificent and powerful, there are not words adequate to describe it. Indeed, any effort to do so would be an attempt to define and describe God, for God *is* love. The omnipotent and illimitable Presence that God is, places Him beyond any form of definition or description.

Thus, if you are to *KNOW* God, to consciously experience His Presence, it becomes necessary that you learn to *turn within* and seek there to gain in your understanding of Him. Through this means, there ultimately shall come into your consciousness a growing realization of the illimitable, holy power of the Presence which lies at the center of your being; and you shall truly see that you are a Child of God, a manifestation of His Presence.

It has been said that one may gain appreciably in this form of endeavor by learning to "Practice the Presence of God." For those who may not understand what is meant by this, a simple explanation, perhaps, would be something like this: That you give as much of your thought, of your understanding, and conscious endeavor as you possibly can muster, over to God. Enter upon each daily activity endeavoring to gain the realization that God is indeed in every facet of your life. See God in everything, in everyone, in every place, in every creature, in all things. Persist in this practice and, sooner or later, you shall find that *you are indeed seeing God in all things.* But, more importantly, you shall have begun to see God *within yourself.*

It is to this end that we seek to lead you onto and along the paths which shall bring this realization to you and into your life. By using the gifts the Father has given you, the gifts of: thought, free will, discernment, judgment and intuition, and the guidance flowing to you from your invisible brethren and the Divine Presence of your Inner Self, you grow in total awareness.

There exists this amazing, yet beautiful, paradox: As you grow in realization of God — and thus of Self — so also do you grow in your ability to give of your love, the Father's love, unto others. And the more this giving of Self is practiced, the greater the power becomes, and the unfoldment of the Spiritual Presence from which this all comes in the first place. Do you not perceive of the beautiful blessings which the Father's love brings into your life? Meditate upon our words, dear brethren, for the deeper meanings they hold for you.

We have placed about each of you a circle of White Light. This is not intended to separate you one from the other. But this is being done that each of you would come to sense to an even greater degree than what you already do, the power of the Christ Light which lies at the center of your being — a beautiful, magnificent, holy, majestic power.

The circle of Light gives you warmth. And, no doubt, you sense its presence. In this form, it is external to your physical being, yet a part of your True Being.

And being thus placed, it allows you a freer opportunity to sense its power as an external power, but which, nevertheless, is a part of and indeed connected to the same Presence that is within your being.

Moreover, being in the form of a circle, it symbolizes the universality of its being and of its nature.

And, if you but use the power of your mind and seek to extend the circumference of its circle, you find that you may indeed do this. And, by this power of thought, you may cause it to reach out and enfold and bring within its perimeter all to whom you would care to reach.

Even now, as we speak these words, you experiment and find that you can take within your circle of Christ

Light everyone to whom you project your thoughts, whether near by or far away.

As you work with this you find, somewhat to your amazement, perhaps, that you can reach out and take within this Light whomsoever you will, and wheresoever they may be; being limited only by the limitations of your consciousness and of your mind.

Perhaps you have not realized, at least not in this aspect, the vastness and the fullness of your power to do this. But this is true.

With the power of the Christ Light you already have within you, and which is your essence and substance, you may reach out to anyone and enfold him within it and give to him the blessings of the Father's love.

This is a beautiful power and a beautiful gift. Now, it is for you to use it and to employ it; not just occasionally, but frequently, joyfully, and with divine purpose and motive; and not just to exercise the power, but in order to give of the Father's Grace and Love unto all you may possibly reach.

The power of the Infinite, upon all realms of the spirit, is limitless. And for the mind, it is limited only by the limitations of the human mind, and only so limited.

This is why it always is a good idea to practice using this power of the Infinite, which is entrusted to you, to bless, to heal, to give of love to one another — the Father's love which enfolds and holds each of you within Its Light.

We would suggest, dear brethren, that you use this technique of the Circle of Light as part of your meditations. If you do, you shall find there are no limitations as to how far you may reach with your mind, especially as a disciple of the Christ Light.

Everyone you touch shall be blessed. They shall receive healing when the Light is used for that purpose. Use this power, and you shall find great joy and fulfillment.

And now, we employ our own suggestion and place about you a circle of the beautiful Christ Light, enfolding you within the power, the warmth and the strength it gives. Let this flow through you, indeed, let it become a part of your consciousness. Sense its vibration, its power and the sustenance it gives you. It is the power of God's Love being made manifest unto you.

It is our prayer that you shall manifest this power unto others. Indeed, it is your responsibility to do so; and, by and through the Grace of the Father, you shall.

Chapter 17

TRUTH AND LIFE

And the truth shall make you free.

T HROUGHOUT the ages man has been in continuous quest and search for truth. And for most men it has seemed to be, in great measure, illusive, fleeting, and beyond their grasp. One may, therefore, suppose that, this being the case, ultimately his frustrations would become so great that he would give up his search in desperation and despair. And were man the insignificant creation, which a number believe themselves to be, this likely would be the result.

But man is not such a simple or insignificant creature. Indeed, the proclamations identifying man as a Child of God, a part of God, are not empty words. The Apostle Paul makes the point that as an heir you are joint heirs with the Christ and inherit, as indeed you already possess, the treasures of the Father's kingdom.

The Presence of the Father, the Presence of the Christ within, indeed, the true and pure essence of your soul, forever burns as a beautiful white light, even though you may, by your own will and conduct, be cast out into darkness. It shall never become extinguished. It always remains aflame and is the source of the driving force which brings about the eternal indwelling longing after truth.

It is difficult for teachers and writers to find the words, or the way to state them, which adequately and simply define what truth is. There are many who would argue that it cannot be defined precisely, for it is a nebulous sort of thing; at least, when one considers man's inadequacy to comprehend it or to recognize it when it is placed before him. In many respects, man's quest for truth is made more complex because of the approach he takes towards it.

Truth is dynamic. A statement setting forth a principle of truth is often the only way it may be presented, but so long as it remains only in the form of written or spoken words, it remains ineffective and its real purpose is lost. It is when that truth is given life through man's using and living the guidance and precepts flowing from it, that such truth really becomes the truth it is. Thus, we would say that all thought, word, or deed which brings peace and harmony, light and understanding, equality and justice and fairness, and which seeks to manifest love in one's life and motivates one to live in such a manner as to bring only these things forward in their life, is truth being made manifest.

You are spirit. You are energy. Therefore, within you there always exists an urge or need for movement and action. Indeed, you may describe yourself as being a moving dynamic force. You are indeed a creation of God, but not merely the creation of a form or nebula of energy which is to merely exist or remain static.

Rather, you are a creation through which God manifests His Presence. You are of God, and all that which is of God must, and shall, manifest the God Presence. And that which is of God is of the power of God which is also imbued with the power of creation. And we do not speak only of the power given to you as human beings to procreate human life. No, dear brethren, the power of creation of which we speak is far greater than even this great power. It would be well for you to take these thoughts into your meditations.

We speak of these things along a serious vein, for they are of that nature. But, at the same time, you must also recognize that while these matters are of a serious nature, they are also cause for great joy, and praise and thanksgiving to the Father-Mother God for the place He has given us all in His creation. Life is meant to bring you the experience of joy, even in the face of much travail, hardship and suffering. For, as you learn to know and to understand the depth and meaning of what we have given you here, you can overcome life's obstacles and find and experience great joy within. For there, deep within, burns the eternal light, the light of all understanding, the light of peace, "the peace which surpasseth all understanding," for there is where God is!

The life of the Beloved Master Jesus has brought a blessing which endures for you, as it does for all who have lived upon this planet since that life and have sought after the truth revealed and taught by Him.

As you seek after understanding, knowledge and greater insight into the true values of life, indeed, the reality of which you are a part, you cannot help but have close contact with *ALL* that the Beloved Master brought into revelation.

It is unfortunate, in a sense, that you do not have available to you the record of the many other experiences and teachings revealed in that incarnation, but which are not recorded in your Bible. And since the record is not complete in that sense, there must be yet another way for you to gain those truths.

Thus it is that we, who come in this light, teach you to carry out certain practices such as meditation and prayer, giving as much study and thought as possible to spiritual matters.

These techniques and practices have purpose. A principal one being to bring forward into your consciousness as fully as possible these truths from the Christ, that they may be brought into manifestation upon the Earth-plane of life.

Obviously, we wish for you to study the teachings we bring you. And we also encourage you to seek out and to study all teachings which flow from the Christ and to which you may be led.

Indeed, my beloved, you are charged with this responsibility: To gain understanding of truth and to live what it teaches you. Yes, dear brethren, this you must do for the Father and for yourself. And no one may perform this obligation for you.

You learn to discern, to select, and to follow that which, to your heart, your mind and your soul, represents truth. And, as you move through this process, you observe an interesting enigma.

As you gain a new perception or insight into some aspect of truth, or a concept takes on a new meaning, or you find that you now clearly understand more about a principle which previously had little or no meaning or significance for you, you discover that even though this new awareness brings a wonderful feeling of joy and a sense of achievement, there remains within you an enthusiastic urge to continue in your quest and move on beyond your new found vistas to discover others which your Inner Self knows lie beyond the present horizons of your consciousness.

And it is wise that you do continue your quest, beloved brethren, because truth is a continuing revelation, bringing you an ever growing awareness and spiritual unfoldment. It never stops, but goes on and on, becoming more beautiful and bountiful with each new experience. And should it not be this way? For it is the Light of the Father's love, the Christ of your being which, because of your unfoldment, is becoming ever more radiant.

The experiences of the Master Jesus leading to His death on the Cross are filled with much meaning. Many symbolisms are represented and used, each one carrying a profound revelation for you. For they depict those experiences which are also necessary to your own life's experiences. Perhaps you already have in some measure experienced some of them. In any event, there is that part of you which must be crucified that the Real Self, the Presence you are, may move upward and forward.

We do not at this moment delve more deeply into these symbolisms, for we have previously taught upon them. Moreover, we would rather have you study carefully the accounts of this event and draw from it your own impressions. Take this into your meditations frequently, for you shall be beautifully blessed by the new understandings that shall be revealed to you.

This experience was a magnificent triumph and initiation for Jesus, as it someday shall be for you. View it with enthusiasm, seeking to gain from it every teaching that it has to give to you. For, as you seek, so shall it be revealed to you. Perhaps not as quickly as you would like, but, as you persevere, you shall gain the understanding you are presently meant to have.

This is a profound time in your life. Each of you has come a long way, beloved brethren. And while there is yet a very long way to go, your Path is traversed only a step at a time; experience by experience, thought by thought, word by word, deed by deed, and with each such step you grow. Be joyful in your experiences, reaping from them the beautiful harvests they bring to your soul.

Life is a continuing, ever flowing, never ending process. As we have stated earlier, there is always change. For life is not meant to be static, in any respect. There may be occasions when, through the will and choice of the individual, progress may be very slight. Indeed, there may even be a regression in certain aspects because of wrongdoing or mistakes or misunderstanding. But even these experiences bring about change, and, in due time, these changes serve to bring about improvement and growth.

The law of Cause and Effect, while demanding and precise in its function, is one of the more important principles underlying the evolutionary changes occurring in man's spiritual progress. Indeed, were this not the case, man would, perhaps, spend even more of his existence going in the wrong direction. For there would not then be the self-imposed disciplinary processes to help place him upon the Path of Light, or to keep him there once he has found it.

While an effect may be one of suffering, even to the point of being of an extreme and severe nature, such as a terminal illness or other form of soul confrontation, there always is presented an opportunity for an understanding and acceptance of all that this principle teaches. That is, that each one may become aware of the beauty of God's love, and realize that through His love, God has given unto man this profoundly just and fair means by which he changes his life from darkness to light.

Thus, we consistently place before you the truth of how it is that each moment of your life, each event coming into your life, each act in which you participate or help bring about, each thought you express, each word you say, all these things, individually and collectively, serve an ultimate good purpose. Even that which is evil shall eventually be corrected and transmuted into good.

So, when you experience suffering or illness, try to understand that these happenings are a manifestation of the operation of divine law in your life. That these events are happening because of causes, whatever they may have been, that went before, and they are now being met and the debts they created are being paid and, hopefully, fully satisfied and discharged.

Thus, you come to realize that you are indeed given a beautiful life—a gift from the Father—which presents every possible opportunity for the richness of fulfillment. Yet, fulfillment cannot be reached without the experiences that such life, of necessity, brings you.

All that which flows from the Father is good and beautiful, and is given in love. Indeed, they are all a part of His love, as are you. And, through the life eternal you have been given, you shall reach the level of perfection which it is your destiny to manifest. This is what you seek after. Therefore, let your hearts be ever thankful. Let your gratitude manifest itself freely and openly. Let your hearts sing praises unto the Father-Mother God Who blesses you and gives you His love in great abundance.

This is a part of the message of love that the Christ Jesus brings to you, my beloved: The Love of God. And this love, dear brethren, can be nothing less than the beauty which it is, nor be without the grace and the power it brings you and gives to you, all of which it is yours to behold and to receive.

And it is your gift, but there is the requirement that you take it in the fullness with which it is given. For truly it is your inheritance. So why do you linger or hesitate? Why do you delay your journey in truth? Only you can give answer to these questions. You shall find your answers within your heart.

We reach to you and touch you and place within you this gift of the Father's love which flows through us unto you. And we bless you in the name of the Christ.

Chapter 18

AT-ONE-MENT

He that hath seen me hath seen the Father.
(John 14:9)

Lift up your hearts unto the Father-Mother God;
open them to His love and receive the great abundance which always flows from Him. Receive of this
blessing, my beloved brethren, for it is yours. Always,
as you turn your thoughts to God and let your heart
dwell upon Him, the blessings which ensue are most
profound.

You realize this, to a degree, and you find that the
more you endeavor to follow this practice, the greater
that realization becomes. Indeed, slowly, but positively,
you find that with each increase in your ability to realize
this you reach nearer the ultimate realization: The reality of the relationship you have with God — and thus with
all life — at-one-ment with Him.

The principle of at-one-ment is not new to you. It is an
aspect of the Ancient Wisdom which has long been given
to all who seek after truth. Many are the teachings which
have been given upon it, and this has been of great value
and help to many seekers. But, in other ways, such teachings have served to delay acceptance of the principle
itself.

By this we mean: Through speaking of "at-one-ment"
as something to be realized in the future, there is the
natural tendency to look upon it as a relationship which

necessarily does not already exist, it is something that is going to come about in the future. Thus, belief in the doctrine of duality, or in separation from God, which has prevailed too long in far too many teachings and philosophies, is given added emphasis, at least indirectly, if not directly.

The idea or concept that you are separate and apart from the Father, that you are an individual being separate and apart from all others, that each is an individual entity and in no way a part of the other encourages and continues to postulate the very beliefs we seek to overcome. You always have been One with the Father. It is your lack of understanding of this reality which is responsible for your present beliefs.

It is fortunate that you have more of an understanding of this principle than others may have, but it is imperative that you gain in the deeper understanding that: The relationship of Oneness is already a fact, you are a part of the whole, a part of the Father and of all His Creation. At the moment you represent an individualized expression of His Divine Spirit but you are not separated from Him.

The Divine Presence which is all about you, indeed, which permeates every facet of Creation, is with you and within you, as you are of It. This principle has been related to you many times and in many forms. And most of you find little difficulty in understanding and accepting it at the intellectual level. But we find that you have difficulty understanding it to the extent of taking it into the inmost depths of your being. Hence, we find this need to dwell upon this teaching.

In fact, it would be well if you would at this very moment ask yourself, "How fully do *I* understand this principle, this truth? Have *I* learned and accepted it to the degree that I can truthfully say: I really *KNOW* this for the truth that it is? That I am of God?

To help you gain your answer, we would have you look to an aspect of this principle. In your studies, and consideration of the teachings we, and others, have made available to you, you have been given insight into the problems growing out of the concept of "duality" of being. At the same time almost, it seems, you have received teachings pointing out that you ultimately must grow beyond that concept to the acceptance of and belief in the superior and absolute principle of Oneness or At-one-ment with the Father-Mother God.

Thus, it is perhaps easier for you to see why there generally is a period during which most "seekers" find themselves somewhat confused by this seeming conflict in philosophy and concept. If you are confused by this approach to this principle, remember this: Because of the very nature of the level of life which you have attained and understand it to be, the principle or concept of "duality" necessarily demonstrates itself. The levels of consciousness in which you are presently living and manifesting yourself are necessarily affected by this concept. It may even be said that it is a part of what you are able to comprehend. And to grow above this in your understanding, you must necessarily first have had to contend with it and to know it for what it is.

Thus, you learn to know yourself as an individual expression of God, of His Presence, of His Power, and of His Love in human, personalized form upon a plane of life to which you must, of course, give some credence or else you would fail to accomplish the very purposes for which you have taken this life. Obviously, this concept must, therefore, also be substantially correct, so far as it goes, and it is.

Perhaps, by now, you recognize that there is a mystery associated with this aspect of life which, in some respects, is comprehendable at the intellectual level but loses its definition as you attempt to resolve it only at that level.

A suggestion we would give, which should carry you a long way towards resolving any dilemma you may have concerning an understanding of this principle, is this: Without concerning yourself as to why things would be this way, simply look upon yourself as the Child of God that you are, in human form, seeking as best you know how to express the Father's Will in your life. With this knowledge, and accepting this relationship in that form, face your earthly problems and the challenges of your daily living *KNOWING* that you are equipped to cope with whatever comes before you, and that you are never presented any obstacle, or opportunity, beyond your capabilities. Be practical and courageous, fortified with the attitude and the knowing that the Father gives you whatever power, wisdom and strength necessary to accomplish every such task well.

As you carry on in this way, knowing and trusting that you are fulfilling your purposes of life in accordance with God's law, you shall find that in time the "realities" of the Earth life — to the extent that they may be real and appear real — pass away and are replaced by the realization of the Realities of the Divine Presence. Thus, that which is Real, regardless of the plane or dimension upon which they may manifest, becomes attainable to you.

Perhaps this solution may appear to be far too simple for understanding a complex and difficult concept and principle. But we would assure you that it is wise to use the more simple approach to solving problems which may become unduly complex and difficult. We have seen many dear brethren get caught up in protracted debates and analysis of various aspects of this principle which have only served to add to their confusion concerning it.

Therefore, we suggest you use the simplest approach you can make to any problem or challenge you may face. If you do this and, at the same time, utilize and build upon the strength of your faith and knowing that God's Presence is indeed within you and available to you, *and use His Presence and His Power,* all things shall be possible for you and you shall do well.

You may find this difficult to grasp and to understand. Were you to go among those who are not familiar with these principles, and the meanings and teachings we give you on them, and speak to them of your Oneness with God, they would likely ridicule you and charge you with blasphemy. But remember the teachings of the Beloved Master and hold to the truth they reveal to you.

Ultimately your understanding shall increase to a full realization of what all this means. During the meantime, it would be well for you to meditate frequently upon this principle and listen carefully to what comes from within. Thus, shall you be guided to follow the path best suited for your progress in this direction.

We call you brethren. We also call you Children of God. This alone demonstrates the existence of the familial ties between us. Indeed, all of us together are at one with each other and with the Father.

In time, my dear brethren, you shall gain the level of understanding and consciousness attained by the Beloved Master. Then, shall you truly know and freely speak, as does the Master: "I and my father are one . . . the Father is in me, and I in Him . . . he that hath seen me hath seen the Father . . . Believest thou not that I am in the Father, and the Father in me? the words that I speak unto you I speak not of myself: but the Father 'that' dwelleth in me, He doeth the works."

Look to the Father for all things. Turn within, for you shall find Him there.

The Beloved Master also proclaims: "And I, if I be lifted up from the earth, will draw all men unto me." The significance of this is made clearer through the realization of the principle of Oneness. Indeed, its significance extends to each of you. As you are "lifted up" in consciousness, so, too, will you draw others unto you.

As you reflect upon the principle of Oneness, and gain greater insight into its application to all life, especially to your relationships with your fellow man, you are better able to accept the significance of what the Master is saying to you with these words.

We would recall to your minds a fact you must not overlook: You are a member of a group of souls, which, much as a large family, has been together for a long, long time. And as one of your number is lifted up in consciousness all others in the group also are lifted up. Conversely, as one of the group misuses his powers, the others are also adversely affected. For you have learned, and now are aware of the fact, that whatever you send forth is your responsibility. And its effect, good or bad, is not necessarily limited to your immediate environment.

It is important that you remain alert to the responsibility you owe both to yourself and to all the members of your group—indeed, to all the universe—to guard carefully the nature of your thoughts and actions.

As you evolve and unfold the Higher Self of your being, the power and the level of the Light you issue forth increases and all your fellow men are lifted up by it. Correspondingly, your area of responsibility is also increased, but your willingness to accept it is readily forthcoming, as is your ability to cope with it increased.

Perhaps you have gained from what we say here the inspiration to seek to understand more fully the implications included in these words and teachings of the Beloved Master. Indeed, to be lifted up in awareness and understanding is to be brought onto new levels of life not previously evident or comprehended by you. May you persevere in such purpose.

A MEDITATION ON AT-ONE-MENT

You find yourself situated in a vast open area which is very desolate. Indeed, it is much as a desert. Very little vegetation appears upon the surface and the temperature is quite warm. The sun is directly overhead, its rays beating down upon you. You are without food or drink. Your thirst is great. Your hunger is great. You find your strength ebbing from you, and you know that unless some miraculous help is forthcoming you cannot exist in this state much longer.

Realizing this, you turn within. And, for a moment, perhaps it is a long moment, but this really doesn't matter, you are clearly aware of the need to do this: To turn to the Father, to His Presence which is within you. But, strangely, along with this thought comes an accompanying realization that you have a choice as to how you shall do this. Shall you turn to God in an attitude and state of complete despair, in fright and with a deep fear of an impending confrontation with the experience called ''death?'' Or, shall you turn to God *knowing* that you shall not only find Him there, but knowing also that whatever comes from this experience shall be in accordance with His law, as it *must* apply to you and to the purposes involved, and with an attitude of appreciation and gratitude for the opportunity to have gained this experience? With this state of mind, you ask for help, guidance and sustenance.

Now, dear brethren, from this moment forward, let the vision unfold for you of whatever may ensue from the choice you shall have made for yourself. We ask you to pause for a time that you may complete your meditation accordingly.

Now, softly and gently, bring your attention back to this level of consciousness.

We have given you this meditation for several purposes, some of which you already recognize. But, perhaps, the paramount purpose has been to impress upon you the tremendous importance of your gaining in ability to meet those moments when you are compelled to face up to those extremely difficult situations your earthly life may bring you.

Obviously, the best way to confront any such circumstance is immediately to enlist the Higher Self of your Being, the God Presence within, and rely explicitly upon the powers and insights flowing from It. But how many follow this practice?

Think back to some of your more recent difficult experiences. Did you not endeavor to cope with them entirely upon the human level? And, if so, you found that your efforts were less than completely successful until you realized the need to reach inside yourself to the God Power within you.

It is not at all contrary to good spiritual practice to daily give conscious attention to this practice. That is, to always turn to this Source of strength, whatever the circumstances which may confront you, serious and difficult, or not. The principal idea is to become so accustomed to doing this that it becomes an automatic reaction for you.

For you see, beloved brethren, we again bring to your attention and consideration the fact and the truth that man only brings good into his life through the constant conscious practice of the God Presence. Unfortunately, most religious practices have led most people to believe that it is only during times of difficulty and untoward situations that they should call upon God or seek to invoke His Power and His Presence.

But we teach, dear ones, that it is far better for you, and for all men, to invoke the Father's Presence in all things. Indeed, consciously make God a part of every facet of your life, in whatever you think, in whatever you desire, and in whatever you do. Thus, you rest your actions, of whatever nature, upon a foundation of what is best for all.

As you reflect upon this, you cannot help but see what a blessing your life shall be, and of the beautiful fruit you shall harvest from your tree of life. For as you sow seeds of the good which flow from the Father's Presence, shall you not also harvest the fruits thereof? Indeed you shall!

Chapter 19

INNER HARMONY VERSUS
THE WORLD OF CONFLICT

*If ye then be risen with Christ seek those things
which are above. . . .* (Colossians 3:1)

You may find yourself wondering about the wisdom
of all the "hurry up" and the fast pace of living and
and doing things that seem to be invading every
avenue of physical life — the relentless enthusiasm for get-
ting everything developed into a condition for "instant
use."

For example, you have "instant foods," "instant
methods" of tending after household and personal needs;
the advance of modern technology seems to be outstrip-
ping man's ability to keep up with it. Indeed, all this
sometimes seems to be both bewildering and frightening,
especially when its pace is contrary to old fixed ideas and
ways. And those who want to hold on to their less speedy
way of life are called "old-fashioned."

But, in spite of the conflict and disruption of personal
habits this process of change brings about, the whole pattern is not really anything new. Historically, man has
been going through this process since the beginning of his
existence and he shall continue to be involved in this process for the balance of his life.

While the forms of change may differ substantially,
relatively speaking, the pattern of the process is always
the same. This Law of Change, if we may call it that, is

as immutably effective as are all other principles and laws of Divine Origin.

We do not mean to say that we agree with all the changes that are occurring upon your plane of life, or that they are good for you and your well-being. But we do say that this process of change, the development of "new" ways of processing foods, manufacturing clothing, building structures and vehicles, and so on, is nothing more than an outworking of man's inherent drive to grow and to develop his intelligence, wisdom, skills, and understanding. Admittedly, however, the major force of these endeavors is directed only to the physical and external aspects of his life, whereas greater interest and endeavor towards spiritual development would be preferable. Even so, these processes do ultimately bring about their learning opportunities through which each one may add to his spiritual awareness.

We make this reference to these earthly conditions for two principal reasons.

The first has to do with the matter of speedy development. There are far too many persons offering classes and courses of instruction which, in effect, guarantee "instant" spiritual development. They may not present their position or approach in that light, but, essentially, that is what they are saying or leading their adherents to believe and to expect.

Similarly, most everyone whose Inner Light has quickened him into undertaking a search for spiritual truth becomes caught up in a vortex of irresistible force, often compelling in its drive, that causes him to seek after and to gain all the knowledge and experience possible in the shortest time possible. Indeed, his enthusiasm frequently overpowers his sense of good judgment and common sense. Hence, the tendency to follow a course of action designed to bring rapid spiritual development and unfoldment is present and ripe for commitment to that purpose.

We do not tell you that you should not be enthusiastic in your spiritual quests, nor are we attempting to discourage you from making as expeditious as possible your endeavors therein, but we are asking you to be as judicious as you can in what you do and in the choices you make. That is, that you weigh carefully the choices presented to you, endeavoring to choose those paths which are most likely to bring you the most good from the standpoint of bringing your life into the bounds of those principles enunciated and taught by our Beloved Master, Jesus the Christ.

Almost always the student finds himself challenged by the fascination and attraction of the psychic experiences which may begin to appear at this time, for they can provide an eager desire to concentrate upon their development. This aspect of his nature is especially one to which the "instant" development processes are directed, and the temptation to follow this path can be very great.

To make the choice to concentrate upon the development of psychic gifts may not necessarily be wrong, however, it is our view—and this is what we teach—that it is best that each one concentrate upon the development and unfoldment of his spiritual Self and the practice of the principles and laws this entails. Thus allowing the psychic gifts to automatically unfold as they are needed and become useful to the spiritual purpose. For this will occur. Indeed, this form of development of the psychic powers is the stronger and more effective way. And it is not fraught with the dangers associated with the course which concentrates only upon the psychic aspects.

But, again, we do not tell you what you must do. We do not force our views upon anyone. The right and the power to make the choices you do are exclusively yours. You have the freedom to choose your course, the path you wish to follow.

To help you in your choice, however, we would point out that every aspect of your spiriual Self, and all the powers that are associated with them, or flow from them, are meant to be developed. And, in due time, you shall develop them. There is a proper time and order for each one to unfold. But you have the power to change this order by the choices you make. If you choose to concentrate upon spiritual purposes, all other aspects shall unfold in due order.

In earlier teachings, we have compared this process with the process of nature employed in the blossoming of a beautiful rose. It first appears as a bud, tightly closed and limited in its form. As it grows and develops, it slowly reaches the point at which each single petal unfolds and opens, in its appropriate order and at its appropriate time, its magnificent beauty for all to see. So, too, are you meant to unfold your true spiritual nature and essence and all the powers that flow from it.

This brings us to the second of our reasons for discussing this particular matter.

It is essential that you recognize and accept the truth of the fact that your true Self, the Higher Self, the Spirit which you are, is indeed an expression of God, manifesting presently as the human being you are. Thus, you occupy a position of substantial responsibility, both to yourself and to your Creator to fulfill your goals, whatever they may be.

Your Inner Self is well aware of this relationship you have with your Creator and your fellow man. Indeed, at that level each one is aware of this fact of being.

What your active consciousness beholds, receives and understands goes to make up what it is. While its ultimate capabilities are essentially infinite, it presently cannot understand those elements of the universe of which it is not cognizant, or of which it cannot perceive intellectually or intuitively. But all that which can now be assimilated becomes a part of your active consciousness.

At the same time, you continue always to be an essential part of the whole of creation which is yet beyond your comprehension and understanding. And what you are, and what you do, necessarily creates its corresponding effect upon all else, even though you are unable to consciously perceive of this occurring.

By being aware of these facts, you perhaps gain further insight into the importance of your need to exercise attention and care to the use of your will—your power of choice. Thus, you learn to use the powers of your consciousness and understanding in the forms and for the purposes designed to be the most fruitful and beneficent for the ultimate good of everyone.

Also, as you do this, you employ your powers in such a way as to give to the Divine Nature of yourself a form in which it may express the Light of Truth which lies within It in a more effective and productive manner. As a matter of fact, you and your fellow man are the primary means through which this Light may be expressed and manifested upon the Earth plane.

When men are in conflict this beautiful power of Truth is misused and perverted to the point that it loses its power for good, or becomes so diluted that it loses much of its effectiveness. On the other hand, it is at such times as this that you who would be Light Bearers, who strive after the conscious living of truth and the total practice of the Principles of Brotherhood as taught by the Beloved Master, can do a magnificent work for the good of mankind.

At this time there is much negative thinking prevalent among many people. And the aggregate of their negative thoughts does much to depress them and others. The Light of God's Power and Strength which can issue forth from you in the forms discussed above touches them, even those who think and live in darkness, and they are helped accordingly.

Do not dwell upon past mistakes. Practice the Law of Forgiveness. Allow its healing power to flow to you and through you unto those to whom you have been bound by your misunderstandings and transgressions. Do not let the debris of the past cover over the Light of your heart. But know that you may profit immeasurably from your past errors by the lessons learned from them. Go forward upon your path with enthusiasm and zeal, yet tempered with compassion, tolerance and patience.

"Put on the whole armor" of Truth. What a bulwark of strength! And it is yours to have and to use. Let this be your choice. Let this be the course your will shall follow that you may truly manifest the Light of the Christ!

Conflict, upheaval, disappointment, frustration, pressures and stresses of all kinds, these define and describe the fruits of man's labor when he only concerns himself with the physical plane, when all his energy, thought and power is directed into external activities and values rather than the internal, inner affairs of life.

Look about you, witness the activities and interests of your fellow man with whom you may work or associate from day to day. You find that it is very rare, indeed, that anyone will even discuss with you, much less practice, the principles which we teach and which you seek to learn and to apply to your daily living.

If you have not thought to make this observation—and mind you, do not do this with any attitude of self-righteousness or superiority, rather, with humble bearing and recognition of the Source of all things—we would suggest you do this.

But, as you make your observations, endeavor also to see that God's laws are certainly at work in your life and in the lives of everyone, in all things. Give recognition to the truth and the knowing that in spite of what may be seen externally, the truth of the matter is that God is *everywhere*. As you have learned, *God IS!* God is within you. You are of God. As the Beloved Master teaches: *"The Father dwelleth within you, He doeth the works."*

So, in all kingdoms, the animal, the vegetable, the mineral, there also is God. There is nothing functioning, or existing, for that matter, that is outside of or without God, for all things are of God.

It is also essential that you be quick to realize your own errors and short-comings. And when you do this, begin immediately to take whatever steps are necessary to rectify them. Employ the principles we have given you concerning this matter of bringing changes into your life where necessary. Thus, you may remain more secure in your determination to reach the goals you have established for yourself.

Expect the new challenges which shall confront you. Adapt to the changes which are brought about in your environment, and especially to those conditions and circumstances which you bring upon yourself.

We concentrate our thoughts in this direction because of the current conditions you witness occurring in the world today. Of course, you are aware of the fact that all things taking place are both demonstrating and manifesting the operation of God's laws—that which is the outworking of past events, and that which presently creates its effects of the future.

It is time for concern, yes. But never lose sight of the wisdom expressed by the beloved Apostle Paul: "Wherefore take unto you the whole armour of God." For have you not learned that all things have purpose; that with God, and through God and by reason of His love, all things work out for the best? Hold fast to this truth, that it may remain strong in your consciousness.

MEDITATION

Now is the time for each one to turn within, to turn to the Inner Self, the True Presence which is there.

In doing so, it is wise to examine and reflect upon what your thoughts have been. In the nature of an experiment, perhaps, we would have you take a moment to review your activities of this day up to this point. Recall to your mind the high points of this day, reflecting upon those experiences which have left the deepest impression with you. As you review them, quickly examine them as to whether they were of a positive nature, or negative in concept and attitude. Were they helpful to others, to yourself, or did they cause harm?

As you have done this, you have, no doubt, come upon the realization that you could have conducted yourself in a more positive and loving manner in one or more of the events reviewed.

We would suggest that you endeavor to incorporate in your daily activity a period devoted exclusively to this practice, preferably in the evening as you are preparing to retire. Others have written upon this, suggesting that this review be done in reverse order. That is, that you review first the most recent of your daily experiences, in point of time to the moment of such review, and then proceed in reverse order taking the events in that order back to the earliest part of the day.

Be as honest with yourself as you possibly can evaluating each event objectively and carefully. Upon those conditions in which you have produced some form of negative result or vibration or harm, immediately work to correct this condition by selfless prayer. It may be that the conditions are such that direct amends are necessary, unless to do so shall cause more harm, whereupon additional prayer work is helpful and needed.

We assure you, dear brethren, that if you persist in this practice, you shall quickly find that beneficent changes shall be wrought in your behavior and in your relationships with others. Almost immediately you shall notice a more vigilant observation of your thoughts, both entertained and expressed. Obviously, this leads to a more careful choice of words and actions.

Perhaps you have grasped what we are giving you in this exercise. Being an active human being upon the planet Earth, you necessarily are given every form of learning experience peculiar to this plane of life. Included is the common tendency, frequently without realizing it, to subdue or quickly suppress, if at all possible, the memory of unpleasant and harmful events and experiences; especially, those experiences growing out of disobedience to the principles of truth of which you are aware. This is quite a normal human reaction.

But the effects of these experiences are, nevertheless, buried in the subconscious and their ultimate effects, sooner or later, are expressed in some appropriate form in your outer life. Essentially, this phenomenon is a form of the karmic processes. Thus, this form of conduct is still a part of you, the deeper part of your consciousness, and the wrongs it has wrought cannot be corrected by anyone other than you.

So, perhaps, you see what a distinct advantage you gain over this kind of problem by utilizing the practice of daily review. You are thus afforded a practical means for immediate recognition of the wrongs you may have committed and at a time when they can more easily be corrected. By doing this, you keep them from infecting the subconscious strata of your being, so to speak.

The good husbandman who brings forth much good fruit at the time of harvest, has exercised great care to weed out all extraneous growths which would seek to invade his fields and lands and take the sustenance meant for the seeds he has planted. Indeed, all tares and thorns are quickly removed so that they may not take hold.

This same principle has application to your behavior, to the fruits of your heart and mind. Remember always, beloved brethren: "As you sow, so do you reap." What seeds you plant shall produce their fruit. Weed out the tares and the thorns that the fruits of your harvest may be sweet and pure, blessed by the love of our Father-Mother God.

Chapter 20

PRACTICING BEING THE LIGHT

Let your light so shine.

(Matthew 5:16)

That ye may be the children of light.

(John 12:36)

But he that doeth truth cometh to the light that his deeds may be made manifest, that they are wrought in God. (John 3:20)

ALTHOUGH your physical eyes cannot see the beautiful phenomenon which flows from prayers, your soul does see it and knows it for the beautiful spectacle that it is. Indeed, at this moment we invite you in your mind's eyes to see yourselves gathered together in the center of a circular edifice, the ceiling and roof of which is of a dome-like dimension.

As you bring this vision into the reality of your mind, you observe that this structure appears to be constructed of a very bright and beautiful substance. It is white, yet it is translucent and pure in its brilliance. And suddenly the realization appears: It is light — the divine light of the Father — and you are in His Holy Temple, a temple built of His Light. And the warmth and the peace that it gives is beautifully uplifting. Indeed, you find that you are each one melting into and with the other; that you — the reality you are—has joined together, each with the other, into a single *ONE* with the Father and the Beloved Lord Christ.

Being filled with this realization of truth and BEING, refreshed and lifted up in feeling and in consciousness, you return to your physical being. But as you do so, you find that the Temple of Light becomes individualized, that is, each of you takes a part of its Light with you. And with this experience comes the meaning of the truth that "ye are the temple of God, and the spirit of God dwelleth in you."

We have carried you through this experience—for it has been your experience of the reality that it is—that you would indeed know, sense and feel this truth which we teach you. And having had this experience, having been given this opportunity to view yourself as you truly are, we would suggest you make the commitment to yourself to give more conscious awareness and expression to the teaching and commandment of the Master: "That ye love one another." And, indeed, "Do unto others as you would have them do unto you."

How beautiful this is! How profound and far-reaching is this simple truth! Were it practiced to the slightest degree by all men, what a tremendous change would be wrought throughout all the world.

And lest you say, "Yes, we know this, but how futile it is. What is there we can do? Just the few of us, there is so little we can do. Why should we even try?" But we say, beloved brethren: BY ALL MEANS *DO* continue in your prayers!

If you could only witness from our point of view how powerful and beautiful a sincere selfless thought and prayer of love is, how such a prayer of love, given in love, is an act of love contemplated by the commandment of the Lord Christ, you would not hesitate a single moment to give repeatedly of yourself in such service.

Remember the teaching of Sodom and Gomorrah—of the power of the prayers of but a few. You are not alone, you are never alone. Especially when you give of thought and effort to the giving of love to others, immediately a great host of your invisible Brethren of Light are drawn to you and they join with you in this purpose.

Such acts of love is God being made manifest in both your life and in the lives of those to whom such love is directed. And this, dear ones, is what you are meant to do and to be.

Know this! Know that as you send your love out into the universe, the light of your love blesses every creature, every soul and being touched by its rays of light. But do not let any thought of self, or of what you may receive from having done this, enter into this purpose at all. For, to allow this is to diminish and take from the quality of that which you have given.

Now, look above you and see the light—the beautiful white light in the form of the Cross of Love which enfolds you and holds you in the bosom of the Father. For you see, as we have been giving you these teachings, your dear invisible brethren have been giving and sending you their love, blessing you, and knowing you for who you really are: Children of God, as are we all His Children of Light.

And now it is your turn to give this love unto everyone.

The light of the Christ is so beautiful and radiant when it is given the opportunity to show forth its presence. And when this occurs, there also is brought forth a magnificent power—indeed, the Christ power, which we would at this moment characterize as being absolutely beyond description from the standpoint of its purity and substance and color.

It may be difficult for you to conceive of its light as being white. But, for the purpose of seeing it as a substance, perhaps this will aid you and allow you to have a better understanding of what we describe.

If you would, assume for a moment that you are looking at a brilliant white light shining all about you. Light,
as you understand it to be, would not be visible. That is,
the ray of light itself is invisible, except for that which is
reflected from some object upon which it is directed.
But, for this teaching, we ask that you envision its
presence. And when this occurs, there also is brought
forth a magnificent power — indeed, the Christ power,
in a form so pure that every object upon which it shines
becomes transparent and translucent. You observe that if
you place a discolored or soiled object or substance
within its ray, it is immediately purified and made clean.

And of itself, it begins to radiate — not just reflect, but
radiate — a similar light. Do you see this? Do you not
perceive of the beauty of this power?

Now, place yourself into this beam of light. As you do
so, you see that you, too, are becoming translucent,
transparent. All that is dross disappears and is carried
away. And, lo, you see that nothing remains but the
light. What you are now seeing is yourself, the light you
are, a Child of the Father-Mother God.

This, my beloved brethren, is your essence. This is
your heritage, your inheritance. Indeed, this is your being in its true state.

Now, as you step from this beautiful Christ light into
the light of the world, you find yourself clothed with the
being you recognize as the incarnation you presently
represent. And, although you may not see the light as we
would have you see it, that light, nevertheless, remains as
we have described it, it is there within you. Indeed, *you
are it!* And your light is one and the same with all the
others, all are a part of each other, and all are a part of
the Father.

We would suggest, my beloved, you contemplate what
we have said, using these visions and ideas we have
helped you to create, that you may better understand
who you are. Meditate upon this and you shall find an in-

creasing and growing ability to even more clearly see what we have meant to place before you.

Open yourselves to the power of God's grace and let it flow through you, through you unto others. This, dearly beloved brethren, is the key to open every door leading to the Light.

⊕

A Meditation:
"The Temple of Light"

We would have you work with us in building a "Temple of Light." There is an importance to this as it shall serve as a means of reaching others who may have many doubts as to their purpose in life.

We ask that you relax completely your physical being, and remove from your mind every thought other than the one thought: "I *know* that I am light and that there lies within me the beautiful majestic white light of the Christ Spirit, and that I may consciously give of this light, which is my love, unto others."

We now call upon you to also use this light to mold and to build this, your "Temple of Light." Concentrate this energy into the form of the temple which represents to you the most holy of places. As you do this, a temple of great beauty is formed, and you find yourself within it.

Now, bring to your mind your concept of the Beloved Master Jesus. He appears before you and extends His hand to you, that you would touch His presence in this way. As you take hold of His hand, you feel the great flow of energy from the Christ to you, and from you to the Christ. You observe the brilliant radiance of His being becoming even more brilliant and radiant. Indeed, the light about the Master becomes brighter and brighter and begins to extend farther and farther out from Him until it encompasses everything within the length of your sight. But still the radiance continues to build and build. And, lo, you see that there are many souls coming from the outer reaches of His light to join with the Christ and with you; indeed, a whole host of brethren are coming to join with you.

As the number of souls increases, you witness that the Beloved Master touches and blesses each one with His love, who, in turn, consciously and purposely touches and blesses the others, thus, giving of their love to one another and to the Christ. A halo of light surrounds everyone which also increases in intensity and brilliance as the flow of the energy of their love increases.

The light of the temple, the radiant white light of the love of the Christ, has lit all of space surrounding you and as far as the eye can see, and everyone within its radiance is lifted up and blessed by it.

You also become aware of this: That as you consciously give of your love to the Master, you are also giving of your love unto all others who have come into the light, for you have both sensed and seen the flow of your love reaching to them. Thus, you are able to more deeply comprehend the relationship you have with all others, and with God. You all are of love and are light.

Within the "temple of your being" the light of your love remains ever radiant and brilliant in its everlasting divine essence—the power of God which seeks to be made manifest unto all men. May this purpose of your soul and spirit be majestically and profoundly fulfilled. If this be your will, then so shall it be.

To the extent to which you have given of yourself to this exercise, the light you have created has reached to souls who have long remained in darkness, and who now have direction and motivation to move towards the light of consciousness.

Take of the blessing this brings you, for, as you have given, so shall it be given unto you. This is the law.

We bless you, dear ones, and cover you with our light of love—indeed, the light of the Father's love.

We thank Thee, O God, for the gift of life and for the truths which are given to us. May all men be strong in their quest for this truth. Amen.